FROM TWO
TO ONE

FROM TWO TO ONE

Preparing for a Lasting Marriage

BRENTON G. YORGASON / TERRY R. BAKER / WESLEY R. BURR

Bookcraft
Salt Lake City, Utah

Library of Congress Catalog Card Number: 81-68622
ISBN O-88494-433-6

First Printing, 1981

Lithographed in the United States of America
PUBLISHERS PRESS
Salt Lake City, Utah

*To the thousands of young Latter-day Saints
whose lives have touched ours
and whose ideas have inspired us
as we have penned these pages*

Acknowledgments

The authors wish to express appreciation to all their colleagues at Brigham Young University who have assisted them in the preparation of this book. They also offer thanks to Lee Ann B. Sudbury for her story in Chapter 4.

Contents

The Reading Experience

It is very interesting and yet quite confusing to realize that most books are purchased by someone to be given as a gift and ultimately never have more than the cover opened . . . and that merely to tickle the heartstrings of a friend by penning words of endearment. As authors, it is our hope that this book will become more than a dust collector — yea, even more than merely another book. Rather, it is our hope that each copy will leap into your laps and become truly *an experience in love* for you and your fiancé(e).

While it is true that most books are written with an "expound and expand" approach, it has been our intent to not only teach correct truths and thus increase your understanding but to move quickly over the asphalt of ideas that are so crucial to creating a celestial marriage and to cross the bridge into the valley where you can learn "how to" create a celestial relationship so that as a couple you can eternally govern yourselves and enjoy each other.

So . . . how do you begin?

As you know, there are many ways to skin a cat. There are also many ways to read a book about marriage. You may want to glance at a page or two of this book while you are doing the housework. You may want to read it while waiting for a football game to begin on television, or you may wish to glance at its pages while waiting for your fiancé(e) at the shopping center. These can all be a beginning, as a fire may be ignited, but there are some other options that may be better. For example:

A little at a time

You may want to set aside a certain time each day or each week to read together. It could be each evening for a few minutes or on Sunday morning or afternoon. If you use this approach, read a chapter or so, and then spend some time talking about what you have read. You'll learn more about each other and from each other than you'll learn from the book . . . and it will do some special things for your relationship as you prepare for your marriage.

Aloud . . . together . . . ?

Should we be so bold as to suggest that you could read this book *out loud . . . together?* This is a shocking, unnatural, fidgeting, nervous, unique experience for most, but as authors we suspect that it will become one of the most enjoyable times you will ever have with your partner. Like the kingdoms of heaven, there are at least three different levels of reading the book. The celestial level would be to read out loud, pondering and discussing as you go and doing many of the activities that are suggested. The terrestrial level would be to read silently, alone, but to talk about it together and do some activities. The telestial level would be for each to read it but not follow it up with discussion and activities. To *not* read it: marital darkness.

A final reward

Before you start reading the book, talk about how you want to read it. Think about the above suggestions and select the combination of them that is good for you. And to assist you in successfully completing it, plan some type of reward for yourselves when you finish. Plan a special evening together, a special dinner, etc. — whatever would be exciting and thrilling to you as you finish the last page.

And now, we wish you an enjoyable and rewarding journey as you put your pen to the contract and begin your date. One final word: you will gain so much more from this book as you select quiet, uninterrupted moments together . . . sitting by the fire away from roommates or family or wherever you can be in tune to each other's needs and feelings — enjoying the love you have for each other.

Marriage is ordained of God.
(D&C 49:15.)

1

There is no earthly happiness
exceeding that of a reciprocal
satisfaction in the conjugal
state.
(H. Giles)

An Eternal Commitment

So you're now engaged! If you are normal, you have probably found your emotions higher than a three-ball kite, more nervous than a fly sitting on the lid of a new bottle of strawberry jam, and yet more settled than a week-old bowl of clam chowder. You have possibly found that your relationship has taken on a whole new meaning and that you are no longer a single entity, but are now thought of by everyone as a potentially eternal unit. While it is true that the engagement period is one of testing the relationship, still it is done on a positive note, with the expectations of marriage in the near future.

As you think of marrying someone, especially for eternity, you need to first of all look at marriage. What is it? and what is it supposed to be? Is it merely a convenient social custom? Or is it something that is much deeper, more beautiful and profound?

Marriage is like a large and beautiful forest. It cannot fully be appreciated by only viewing a few of the trees. Rather, you can gain a proper understanding of what marriage is and why the Lord calls it the "new and everlasting covenant" (D&C 131:2) only by stepping back and first examining this forest from a broad spiritual and intellectual vantage point. As you do this, you can begin to focus on such questions as:

What are the purposes of life?

Why are we really on the earth?

Where did we actually come from?

What are the eternal implications that provide meaning and purpose to our lives?

It is only when you find answers to these questions that you will begin to understand what marriage *is* and *ought to be*, and why it is the foundation for eternal exaltation.

Marriage Is at the Heart of the Gospel

The Lord has revealed that the intelligence part of man had no beginning and will have no end (D&C 93:29-38). You are an eternally existing being, pure and simple. You were, however, born in a pre-earthly life as a spirit child of heavenly parents, and you lived for a time as a heavenly family. During this pre-earthly existence you had a spiritual body, and it resembled the earthly body you now have (1 Nephi 11:11; Ether 3:16). Even so, your spirit body did not have the physical elements of flesh and bone. It *was* made of matter, but spirit matter is "more fine or pure" (D&C 131:7) than the matter you know on earth.

You learned many things and had some joy in that pre-earthly life, but you could not have a "fulness of joy" in that condition (D&C 93:33-34). Before you could obtain a fulness of joy, you needed two additional things. You needed (a) a physical body, and (b) the knowledge and skills you could acquire by living in an environment where good and evil were competing with each other (2 Nephi 2:23). A plan was therefore introduced that would allow you to obtain a physical body *and* have the experience with opposition that you would need to prove your eternal worth.

There are several aspects of this pre-earthly condition that can help you understand the central role of marriage. The Gods who were your parents were a married couple (D&C 131:4), and their main goal was to help you and their other children progress and grow. They did this by helping others acquire spiritual bodies, teaching them, creating a home for them (an earth), and helping them progress.

Why do they do it?

What is the purpose of this activity?

What gives it meaning?

These questions, too, have answers. As the scriptures teach, "men *are*, that they might have joy" (2 Nephi 2:25, italics added). It is this *joy* that gives meaning and purpose to life. Your heavenly parents worked at helping you grow so you could experience greater joy, and perhaps through this service your heavenly parents are experiencing their greatest joy. Thus you see that the most joyful of exalted experiences possible is attaining godhood and helping others, and you also see that it is done only as a *married couple*. Without marriage there would be no spirit children (D&C 131:4). There would be no meaning, no purpose, and no joy. There would be no need for earths, and all the beauty in life would not exist.

Thus you see that celestial marriage is much more than a convenient social arrangement or civil contract. It is a sacred and eternal covenant that existed before the foundations of this earth were laid. It is an "order of the priesthood" (D&C 131:2) that is everlasting. It is a holy ordinance that plays the key role in your exaltation and eternal happiness.

Hopefully, these insights help you understand why the Lord, when He was creating the earth, said, "It is not good that man should be alone; I will make him an help meet for him" (Genesis 2:18). These insights should also help you understand why He revealed to the Prophet Joseph Smith that "whoso forbiddeth to marry is not ordained of God, for marriage is ordained of God unto man" (D&C 49:15). They should also help you understand why the Lord emphasizes that celestial marriage can be performed only in special rooms in the most sacred of all places — the temple.

This exalted view of marriage can also help you understand why you cannot be exalted as an individual. You are exalted only as a couple. Section 132 of the Doctrine and Covenants discusses the process of becoming gods, with the entire discussion involving what *couples* do rather than what individuals do. The main verses are 19 and 24. The Lord states that "they shall pass by the angels to their exaltation," and "they shall be gods" and "then shall they be above all." In the preceding section He explicitly taught that marriage is necessary for exaltation:

> In the celestial glory there are three heavens or degrees; And in order to obtain the highest, a man must enter into this order of the priesthood [meaning the new and everlasting covenant of marriage]; And if he does not, he cannot obtain it. He may enter into the other, but that is the end of his kingdom; he cannot have an increase. (D&C 131:1-4.)

This doctrine can perhaps be best understood by making a slight change in the couplet that was coined by Lorenzo Snow: As man now is, God once was; and as God now is, *couples* may become.

What Should Marriage Be Like?

Marriage Should Be a Loving Relationship

Paul counseled husbands to "love your wives, even as Christ also loved the church" (Ephesians 5:25). Jacob also taught that marriage is better when "husbands love their wives and . . . wives love their husbands" (Jacob 3:7). Thus love is an important part of marriage; and when you marry in the Lord's prescribed manner, it should not be for simply a "convenience" relationship. Some marry because a spouse is a needed commodity for their progression and advancement. They "need" a spouse for their profession or in order to be given responsible positions in the Church. Although these may be some of the advantages of marrying, you should love your mate and realize that love is the most crucial dimension of a celestial marriage.

Temple Marriage Is a Style of Life As Well As an Event

Though it is hardly imaginable, some young couples actually

feel that the event of a marriage in the temple is a "fail-safe" assurance of their exaltation. An unfortunate example of this was shared with the authors:

A devoted Latter-day Saint girl fell in love with a not-so-devoted LDS boy. The young man wanted to marry, but the girl insisted she would never be married anywhere except within a temple. To this the boy finally and begrudgingly agreed, and he proceeded to go through the necessary steps to obtain a temple recommend. The date was set, arrangements were made, and the night before the ceremony the boy's fraternity brothers gave him a bachelor's party from which he appeared at the temple the next morning with red eyes and a slight hangover. Even though the girl was aware of the incident, the marriage was performed, and the girl truly felt she had accomplished her goal.

What this girl apparently did not understand is that the marriage ceremony in the temple is an important event that begins (or is a continuation of) a certain style of life. It does not automatically qualify her for exaltation. Section 132 of the Doctrine and Covenants is quite clear about this:

And as pertaining to the new and everlasting covenant, it was instituted for the fulness of my glory; and he that receiveth a fulness thereof must and shall abide the law, or he shall be damned, saith the Lord God. And verily I say unto you, that the conditions of this law are these: All covenants, contracts, bonds, obligations, oaths, vows, performances, connections, associations, or expectations, that are not made and entered into and sealed by the Holy Spirit of promise, of him who is anointed, . . . whom I have appointed on the earth to hold this power . . . are of no efficacy, virtue, or force in and after the resurrection from the dead; for all contracts that are not made unto this end have an end when men are dead. (D&C 132:6-7.)

Elder Bruce R. McConkie gives the following clarification of what it means to be sealed by the Holy Spirit of Promise:

To seal is to *ratify*, to *justify*, or to *approve*. Thus an act which is sealed by the Holy Spirit of Promise is one which is ratified by the Holy Ghost; it is one which is approved by the Lord; and the person who has taken the obligation upon himself is justified by the Spirit in the thing he has done. (*Mormon Doctrine*, 2nd ed. [Salt Lake City: Bookcraft, 1966], p. 361. Hereafter cited as *Mormon Doctrine*.)

The girl whose goal was temple marriage obtained it, but she had not yet achieved the more important goal of a celestial marriage that was approved and ratified by the Holy Spirit of Promise and by the Lord. Verse 8 of section 132 explains why this is necessary: "Behold, mine house is a house of order, saith the Lord God, and not a house of confusion." Thus, in order to begin to qualify as candidates for a *fulness,* couples must be married in the temple. This is only a beginning; however, both partners then need to live worthy to stand justified before the Lord without compromise in their actions.

Marriages Are to Be Eternal

The Savior has indicated that marriages should last forever. He taught this clearly in response to the taunting Pharisees:

> And he answered and said unto them, Have ye not read, that he which made them at the beginning made them male and female, And said, For this cause shall a man leave father and mother, and shall cleave to his wife: and they twain shall be one flesh? Wherefore they are no more twain, but one flesh. What therefore God hath joined together, let not man put asunder. They say unto him, Why did Moses then command to give a writing of divorcement, and to put her away? He saith unto them, Moses because of the hardness of your hearts suffered you to put away your wives: but from the beginning it was not so. (Matthew 19:4-8.)

This scripture reveals that the Lord's highest law is for His children to live in a system where divorce, annulment, and desertion are unknown. He recognizes, however, that in some historical periods the people do not live this very demanding law. When this occurs, He holds this ideal as something to strive toward while allowing His people to live lesser laws that are consistent with their level of progress. This adaptability with regard to divorce is seen in three instances. The Lord gave a lesser law to the children of Israel in the time of Moses since they were permitted to divorce for several reasons (Deuteronomy 24:1-4). Then in the meridian of time He taught His disciples that they ought to live a law that was at an intermediate level. Divorce was to be allowed for fornication, and those who were divorced were not to remarry (Matthew 19:9). The standards that are applied in the Church currently indicate that the Lord is again allowing a lesser law. In certain circumstances He permits remarriages within the temple after a divorce, and couples can have their sealings cancelled when it appears to the First Presidency to be necessary. Thus the Lord values stability but apparently recognizes that it does not always occur.

Marriage Is for Bearing Children

Becoming a parent is the basic reason for marriage. As the Lord has indicated, we should "multiply and replenish the earth" (Genesis 1:28). While we are upon the earth most of us are able to procreate earthly children, and when we do this we are assisting the Lord in the plan of salvation. Later, in our post-mortal life, *if* we have earned the privilege, we will have the opportunity to bear additional children by giving them spirit bodies and helping them progress toward their exaltation.

The process of being parents is not a matter that should be taken lightly. It is at the very heart of the gospel, and will become one of the most important sources of "joy and rejoicing." In one revelation the Lord summarized the glory of exaltation by saying that the glory of it is a "fulness and a continuation of the seeds forever and ever" (D&C 132:19). Listen if you will, to the words of Spencer W. Kimball regarding this issue:

"Be fruitful and multiply and replenish the earth." The Lord does not waste words. He meant what he said. You did not come on earth just to "eat, drink, and be merry." You came to get yourself a mortal body that could become perfected, immortalized, and you understood that you were to act in partnership with God in providing bodies for other spirits equally anxious to come to earth for righteous purposes. And so you will not postpone parenthood. There will be rationalists who will name to you numerous reasons for postponement. Of course, it will be harder to get your college degrees or your financial start with a family, but strength like yours will be undaunted in the face of difficult obstacles. Have your family as the Lord intended. Of course it is expensive, but you will find a way, and besides, it is often those children who grow up with responsibility and hardships who carry on the world's work. . . . do not limit your family as the world does. I am wondering now where I might have been had my parents decided arbitrarily that one or two children would be . . . the limit; for

I was the sixth of eleven children. Don't think you will love the later
ones less or have fewer material things for them. Perhaps, like Jacob,
you might love the eleventh one most. Young people, have your
family, love them, sacrifice for them, teach them righteousness, and
you will be blessed and happy all the days of your eternal lives.
(*Marriage* [Salt Lake City: Deseret Book Company, 1978], pp. 22-23.
Hereafter cited as *Marriage*.)

Married Couples Are to Teach Their Children

In addition to bearing children, the Lord has revealed that as
married couples we should rear our children properly. This is His
most emphatic statement about this matter:

> And again, inasmuch as parents have children in Zion, or in any of
> her stakes which are organized, that teach them not to understand
> the doctrines of repentance, faith in Christ the Son of the living God,
> and of baptism and the gift of the Holy Ghost by the laying on of the
> hands, when eight years old, the sin be upon the heads of the parents.
> . . . And they shall also teach their children to pray, and to walk
> uprightly before the Lord. (D&C 68:25, 28.)

King Benjamin also discussed these responsibilities in his great
address by saying:

> And ye will not suffer your children that they go hungry, or naked;
> neither will ye suffer that they transgress the laws of God, and fight
> and quarrel one with another, and serve the devil, who is the master
> of sin, or who is the evil spirit which hath been spoken of by our
> fathers, he being an enemy to all righteousness. But he will teach
> them to walk in the ways of truth and soberness, ye will teach them
> to love one another, and to serve one another. (Mosiah 4:14-15.)

Marriage Prevents Loneliness

There are many reasons for marriage, and while bearing and
rearing children are the central reasons, there are others. The Lord
indicated that another reason is that "it is not good that the man
[or woman] should be alone" (Genesis 2:18; Moses 3:18). Marriage prevents loneliness and provides an opportunity to learn
unselfishness and to work as a team in bringing about righteousness. This is a simple truth, but one which has far-reaching implications.

Marriage Preserves the Patriarchal Order

There are several scriptures which teach that the husband is to preside in the home. At the time of the Fall, Eve was told that her husband should "rule over her" (Genesis 3:16; Moses 4:22). Later, Paul wrote to the Ephesian Saints:

> Wives, submit yourselves unto your own husbands, as unto the Lord. For the husband is the head of the wife, even as Christ is the head of the church; and he is the Saviour of the body. Therefore as the church is subject unto Christ, so let the wives be to their own husbands in every thing. Husbands, love your wives, even as Christ also loved the church, and gave himself for it. (Ephesians 5:22-25.)

The analogy of husbands presiding over wives as Christ presides over the Church provides some clues about *how* husbands should preside. They should do so in righteousness and with a gentle warmth. They should lead with persuasion rather than with force, with long-suffering rather than with a quick temper, with gentleness rather than with toughness, with meekness rather than with an all-knowing attitude, with love unfeigned rather than with love merely verbalized, and with kindness rather than with abrasiveness (Matthew 19:5-7; D&C 121:36-43). *Presiding does not mean that the husband gets his way more than others or that he has the final say. It means that he directs the process in the home.* That is the key phrase in what it means to preside. He guides the process of making decisions and getting proper things done.

Freedom Within the New and Everlasting Covenant of Marriage

You have spent the last few pages discovering the boundaries the Lord has set for marriage. Since He is the same yesterday, today, and forever (D&C 20:12), these characteristics of marriage remain constant even if social conditions change and new innovations or life-styles are accepted in the world. New technologies and social inventions will change most social institutions, such as governments, economic systems, and educational institutions, but they cannot be allowed to alter the basic characteristics of the new and everlasting covenant of marriage.

It is essential to also realize that the "boundaries" the Lord has set for marriage do not rigidly define every aspect of marriage. He has provided the above guidelines and specific limits that define the basic nature of marriage, but His boundaries allow for considerable flexibility in areas that are not fundamental to the marriage. Therefore, each couple has some freedom in deciding what they want their marriage to be like.

One way to look at this is to view marriage as a *stewardship.* The Lord has identified some basic boundaries of this stewardship by giving instructions, such as avoiding adultery, loving each other, being presided over by the priesthood, etc. Then, within these boundaries, couples have the freedom and responsibility to govern their own marital stewardship.

Those who accept the challenge of charting their own course and making their own marital decisions within the bounds set will experience a variety of blessings. They will learn the joy of standing on their own two feet. They will increase their ability to make decisions. They will learn how to create pleasant relationships with others, and they will face the adversities that are inevitable in mortal and post-mortal life. Then as this experience helps them gain more knowledge and intelligence, these skills will rise with them in the resurrection (D&C 130: 18-19) and help them attain their ultimate destiny. But those who look to traditions, leaders, or peers for clear-cut answers to *every* aspect of marriage will find that they become less able to manage their stewardship. As in the parable of the talents, those talents which they have may be taken away (Matthew 25:14-30).

Areas in Which Couples May Make Choices

One of the areas in marriage where there is room for individual variation is in the *amount of independence* a couple has. This independence is not an "all or nothing" situation but is reflected on a continuum having two extremes with many different levels or degrees, as shown below:

Amount of Independence

0	1	2	3	4	5	6	7	8	9	10
None	Very, very little		A small amount			Quite a bit		A great deal		Total independence

It is likely that you would never want to be at either extreme of independence in marriage. If you were completely independent, it would not be a marriage at all. You have not even had that much freedom with a missionary companion or with a roommate in a dorm. At the opposite extreme, you would probably not want to be so closely tied to your spouse that you have no freedom at all. Perhaps you may desire a relationship such as the Halladays', which is illustrative of a marriage with relatively little freedom:

The Halladays

"We have a saying in our marriage: No secrets! We have none, and we love it! We share everything with each other — our thoughts, our disappointments, our temptations — everything. I like to know where she is going when she leaves, and I always let her know what I'm doing. If I'm going to be late, I always call her as soon as I know my plans. Marriage to us means *really* being one."

The Halladays are at level two or three in the previous continuum. They have very little independence, and they prefer this in their marriage. You may desire more independence. This desire for more elbow room is not inconsistent with the gospel ideas, as illustrated by the Channings' life-style. They know the Halladays and, in fact, socialize with them each month as they attend the temple together, spend evenings enjoying special cultural events together, etc. Even so, the Channings are quite different in the area of independence:

The Channings

"I'm a fairly private person. I love to be alone, to think, to read, to meditate, and to plan. We do a lot of things together in our marriage and with the kids, but it is also important to us that we be individuals and have our individuality. This means that we need some separate areas of our lives that aren't really shared. We feel this type of a relationship creates something special that could be obtained no other way, and it is created in the trust and respect we have for each other. I think I am a better wife and John is a better husband than we would be if we were like the Halladays.

Their style is perfect for them, but if we lived that way, it would drive us up the wall."

The Channings' marriage is about a seven on the continuum. They have a great deal of independence, and for them it is healthy and suitable. And so you could ask:

Which marriage is better?
Which couple is more righteous?

With regard to *independence*, the answer is *neither*. This is evidently an area in which the gospel allows for differences. Both couples can retain their own styles and be equally happy and successful. In fact, with their personality differences, they probably need to have their own styles to be happy and have joy. If the couples were to switch life-styles, they would all suffer and possibly fail as a result.

Another area in which couples can differ is in how fast a pace they choose to live. Some couples desire a fast pace; they are always on the run. They like to fill every minute with something. They have a lot of energy, and they find it fulfilling to use it. Other couples prefer a slower pace in which they have more time to relax and, as a consequence, have few demands.

This, too, can be shown on a continuum:

Pace of Life

0	1	2	3	4	5	6	7	8	9	10
Very slow pace		Slow pace			Moderate pace			Fast pace		Very fast pace

Again, are the couples who live a fast-paced life more apt to be keeping the commandments than those who live a slower-paced life? Could the opposite be true? As to the extremes, both are undesirable. Couples who try to "run faster than they can" are unwise stewards, and they would be better off moving at a slower pace. On the other hand, living an extremely slow life is inconsistent with the admonition to "be anxiously engaged in a good cause, and do many things of their own free will, and bring to pass much righteousness" (D&C 58:27). This still leaves plenty of room for differences in individuals and couples. As you consider the perils of being extremists, you should be cautious in placing your marriage relationship below a two or above a nine, but if it feels natural and right you should feel *good* about placing yourselves at any of the points in between these extremes.

There are many other areas of marriage wherein there is freedom *within* the bounds the Lord has set. The following list identifies many of these areas. As you read them, you will no doubt feel strongly about some of the dimensions and not care much about some others. As you examine them, please keep in mind that some preferences are determined by the person you marry. On the other hand, you may feel strongly about some of them regardless of the person you marry. While Church leaders have provided guidelines in some of these areas, each allow for varying degrees of freedom within marriage. *You would do well to examine this list together and have some long talks about what you want your marriage to be like.*

Areas Permitting Flexibility in Marriage

1. How much intellectual stimulation should we provide each other?
2. How much privacy should each spouse have? How much of our life is not known by our spouse?
3. How much affection is expressed physically? How much touching, embracing, kissing, snuggling, etc.?
4. How much affection is expressed verbally? How frequently should we do such things as saying, "I love you" and writing poetry, affectionate comments, tender phrases, etc.?
5. How much time can we spend with close friends?
6. What proportion of our friends should be friends of the couple or of only one individual?
7. How much will personal development be emphasized in the marriage? For the husband? For the wife?
8. How much time should be devoted to Church callings? How much time would be too much or too little for us?
9. How much do we want to travel?
10. How do we want to handle our money?

11.   How often should we visit relatives? How much should we listen to their advice?
12.   How much is it okay for one member to change after the wedding and in what areas?
13.   How shall we handle differences of opinion?

Summary

The purpose of this first chapter has been to place marriage in its eternal perspective — that is, at the very heart of the gospel. You have also become sensitive to a number of specific Latter-day Saint teachings about what marriage should be. These teachings can set boundaries for your marriage, and these boundaries are not negotiable. They are the same yesterday, today, and forever. You should both understand what they are and create a marriage that is consistent with these bounds the Lord has set. Within these boundaries, you have also learned of areas in which you are free to make choices regarding your own relationship. Thus while there is structure to marriage, there is also some freedom for individual and couple differences. This idea is essential if you are to understand and then accept your uniqueness as a couple and as an individual.

You are now prepared to move into the area of your personal readiness for marriage, to determine what you can do during the next few weeks to truly be ready to become "one."

*Becoming the right person
to marry, a task we pursue
in our youth, becomes of
paramount import as we think
of saddling someone with
what and who we are for
eternity.
(Brenton G. Yorgason.)*

2

Preparing for Your Marriage Milestone

Some important questions you each must ask yourself as you consider marrying are: "Am I truly ready for an eternal relationship?" and, "If I'm not ready, what do I need to do to become ready?" While few would agree that a child of ten or twelve is knowledgeable and mature enough to marry, it is also true that some individuals are not ready at twenty or twenty-five. Age is only one factor to consider as you think of moving into "the good life." Being personally ready for marriage is extremely complex because so many factors enter in, including biological development, mental and emotional maturity, financial adequacy, emancipation from parental control, and especially the ability to perform the many new roles that come with marriage.

As a young Latter-day Saint, you have a unique opportunity to consider marriage on a different basis from that of the rest of the world. Those in the "world" who don't understand the eternal role of marriage often view it as a "station" which can be moved in and out of with relative ease as two people find their needs and desires changing. Because of this orientation, people often marry with little attention to their readiness, knowing that they can test their maturity as well as the strength of their relationship without being locked in, without a long-term commitment to each other. Those who know the purpose of marriage realize that an "eternal unit" is being formed, and they need to be ready before they enter it. Incidentally, it is noteworthy that LDS marriages which are performed in a temple show a much lower divorce rate than do civil marriages in the same communities. (*Marriage*, p. 32.) This is probably partly because those who marry in the temple have extended a greater effort toward being personally ready to marry and consequently are more satisfied with their marriage once they are there.

Well . . . where do you begin?

The most important ingredients in any marriage are the two partners who make up the marriage. This union can be no better than the separate individuals involved, and before the partners can begin to understand their relationship, they must first learn to understand themselves. Thus the importance of the saying "Know thyself."

A General Idea

As you consider your personal readiness for "taking the leap," you should remember that marriage brings with it many obligations to perform a myriad of tasks. These tasks can be thought of as (a) relationship tasks and (b) situational tasks. Relationship tasks center around how well you adapt to and perform with and respond to your spouse. You can think of these tasks in terms of your openness, your honesty, your support, your ability to satisfy the needs of your spouse, etc. Situational tasks, on the other hand, deal with providing economically for your family's needs, knowing how to feed your family, knowing how to maintain an orderly home, etc. The lists of both types of tasks are long. The main point here is that marriage is a very involved, complex arrangement, and so you need a large number of skills if you are to create a pleasant and rewarding relationship.

Areas of Personal Readiness for Marriage

As a member of the Church, you are taught to become self-reliant, independent, industrious, and thrifty. The Church is placing continual and increasing emphasis on personal and family preparedness. This has been broken down into six basic categories which you should plan for in your preparation for a successful marriage. These are as follows:

Social, Emotional and Spiritual Strength
Literacy and Education
Career Development
Financial and Resource Management
Home Production and Storage
Physical Health

As you roll up your engagement sleeves and pursue the task of preparing for marriage, perhaps it would be well for you to walk through each of these areas one at a time. This will not only allow you to become aware and sensitive to these areas, but will also assist you in becoming knowledgeable as to what you can *personally do* to improve and grow.

Social, Emotional, and Spiritual Strength

Social, emotional, and spiritual strength are areas that you need to give the most careful consideration, for they serve as the mortar that keeps the other areas strong and stable. Because of the very breadth of these areas, perhaps it would be well to consider each of them separately.

Social strength. It is no dark hidden secret that as a society we are moving at a very rapid pace. Not only does this create an environment of extreme social demands, but it also places a newly married couple in a position of having to skillfully interact with each other. They must do this not merely to survive but also to create a marriage that is both satisfying and rewarding. Thus the need for various social skills.

Perhaps the most basic social skill a person could acquire in preparing for marriage is that of *effectively communicating.* As an engaged couple, you should sit down and communicate about *how* you communicate and about your seeming ability to solve problems together. When two young people are able to express their feelings and emotions to each other, they are then able to effectively cope with the "dishes, diapers, and dollar bill" mainstream of marriage.

In addition to effective communication and problem-solving skills, the acquisition of social skills also involves learning to interact with others in a way that reflects maturity, sound judgment, and a sensitivity toward the ideas and actions of others. Acquiring this sense of social balance is not accomplished by merely reading books; it is developed only as you interact and then as you reflect on *how* you interact with each other. Perhaps this is why so much emphasis is placed on making sure you are ready and making sure you know yourselves well enough to know with what type of person you can create a satisfying and rewarding marriage relationship.

Emotional strength. As you have undoubtedly been primed for years, developing emotional stability is crucial if you expect to enter marriage with the hope of it lasting through the eternities. That is not to say that you can expect immediate perfection in the use of your emotions. You do, however, need to explore how well you understand what goes on in your mind and body as you act upon as well as react to the different forces in your environment.

In considering the base of emotional strength and maturity, there are three separate issues which serve as ideal indices in evaluating your emotional readiness for marriage: age, desire for children, and emotional maturity.

Age: First, what about age at marriage? Is it really related to readiness for marriage? The answer is a definite *yes.* A great deal of research shows that how old you are when you marry correlates very highly with how successful your marriage will ultimately become. Your chances of happiness are greatest when you wait until you are well into your twenties. It is an old wives' tale in our culture that your chances of happiness decrease when you wait until after age twenty-two or twenty-three to marry. Research actually shows that those who marry in their middle twenties have the highest chances of having their marriages last. And this is most consistent with the advice of Church leaders. If you get some education and go on a mission, that puts you into your twenties, and then you are ready to begin thinking about who to marry.

Desire for children: A second barometer of emotional strength is whether you want to become a parent. Some research suggests that your attitude toward having children is related to the probability of being happily married. It is important to know that this desire-to-have-children issue has nothing to do with the number of children wanted or how soon after the marriage they are wanted. The issue is just whether or not the individuals want to have them.

The application of this issue in your personal life is fairly straightforward. If you don't want to become a parent, you are probably also not ready for marriage. Within the framework of the gospel it is inconsistent to consider marriage for time and eternity and yet be so immature or selfish that you do not want to pay the price and receive the blessings of procreating and rearing children. You would do well to sit down as an engaged couple and "talk through" your feelings and expectations regarding having a family.

Ability to control your emotions: Many scholars have suggested that emotional maturity is important in readiness for marriage. Some individuals let their emotions get the best of them in ways that damage or destroy their relationships, as they haven't learned how to control their anger, hurt, despair, jealousy, or frustration. They say things they don't mean and hurt those who are the most important to them. Those who have these problems ought to avoid rushing into marriage, because these traits may destroy it quickly. They ought to take some time to improve their emotional maturity by getting help from others, such as friends, their bishop, or, if necessary, a professional counselor. Above all, they ought to avoid getting married at a young age — say under twenty-one or twenty-two. In some instances, counsel or answer to prayer may indicate the need to get away from their parental homes and get out on their own. They may be much more ready to get married when they are twenty-two or twenty-three and have had some growth-producing experiences in a college or work setting.

Here are some questions relating to characteristics of emotional maturity that make a big difference in marriage:
— Am I flexible or adaptable in my opinions? Can I give in and change my opinions?
— Do I always have to be right, or can I admit my faults and mistakes?
— Can I give to others, or am I always taking from others?
— Can I lift others around me, or am I always cutting them down?
— Do I tend to act on my impulses rather than reason?
— Am I moody, with lots of ups and downs? (Everybody has some, but too many can harm a marriage.)
— Am I afraid to get close to another person?
— Am I afraid to cut the apron strings?
— Do I have enough self-control?

In sum, we have discussed emotional strength as it pertains to marital satisfaction. This was done by examining the three basic indices of emotional strength, which are (a) age at marriage, (b) desire for having children, and (c) ability to control emotions. Although these three issues are not all-inclusive, they do reflect areas of importance as you make ready for your wedding day.

Spiritual strength. You cannot merely announce to the world and to your fiancé(e) that you are "spiritual" and necessarily have it so. In fact, the only way you can achieve spiritual strength is by developing spiritual skills, such as being charitable (unselfish), forgiving, and humble, and by being able to make covenants with the Lord and living in accordance with those covenants once they have been made. While these issues are discussed elsewhere in later chapters, it is good to think of them as part of being ready for marriage.

Literacy and Education

Education is not always the same as years in school. Some

people spend many years in school and get degrees, but they don't get an education. Others learn wherever they are.

There are two basic advantages of an education. The first (although oftentimes not foremost) is that it broadens a person's perspective on life. It is difficult to realize one's potential when one has no understanding of what potential life has to offer. The second advantage of pursuing education is that it helps us acquire skills which allow us to make a greater contribution to society as well as to provide a foundation for a more financially rewarding life. While one could spend a great deal of time discussing the advantages of gaining an education, the purpose of mentioning it here is to simply indicate that becoming literate and furthering one's education gives just that much more solidarity to a young couple beginning married life.

Career Development

Although many consider career development as an area crucial only for the husband, the breadwinner, this is oftentimes misleading and even untrue. Career development is a subject that should be evaluated by both husband and wife, as careers determine so much of a person's life.

Our society has shifted and expanded its expectations and opportunities for women in terms of career development. In addition, Church leaders counsel that preparing for a career will be growth-producing for young ladies and will also provide a vocation for them to fall back on after they are married, should the need arise (with the husband's death or disability, or other circumstances). The Church leaders counsel that, wherever possible, a mother should remain at home with her children. Nevertheless the time may come when circumstances make it necessary for the mother to have outside employment, and you should be prepared for such a possibility in your own marriage.

The need for young men to prepare themselves for careers is obvious in our complex, demanding, and financially oriented society. Those who fail to prepare, who have their sights set low, and who in fact aim from the hip, find themselves struggling for survival both in society and in their own homes.

At this time in your life, as you prepare for marriage, you should become even more aware of your capabilities, your likes and dislikes, and then set short-term goals which will then lead to the attainment of long-range career fulfillment.

Financial and Resource Management

While it is not intended that we delve deeply into the issues of financial resources and management in marriage, it is our intent to sound a fair warning to you as you prepare financially for marriage. Many couples find themselves washed up on the rocky crags of financial ruin because they overextended themselves or because they gave "no thought for the morrow." As you move through the engagement period, it would be well for you to discuss finances and to begin to plan for the needs of tomorrow. Those couples who have a nest egg when they marry (and then who never allow this nest egg to be depleted) do themselves a great favor, as they are never at the end of their financial rope. You would do well to talk to your parents, a friend who is "there," or someone who can give you counsel about the financial awakening you will experience as you return from your honeymoon and land firmly on the soil of today's financial complexities.

Home Production and Storage

Even if you have thought that home production and food storage are not important, as you are planning to live in a small apartment, you should still become sensitive to it. By giving it some thought, perhaps you will be like one young couple who married recently. They knew each other and dated for about six months, and during this time, instead of spending hundreds of dollars on expensive dates, they rechanneled their spending money into food storage. When they married they had an entire year's supply of food in their extra bedroom. Their use of the food storaged enabled them to continue schooling without a great amount of financial hardship. Why, the new husband even gained weight the first year of their marriage!

As you consider your personal situation and your preparedness for marriage, perhaps you can discuss these issues with others, and especially with your prospective marriage partner, and come up with a plan that is suitable to your needs.

Physical Health

In considering the areas of personal readiness for marriage, this section stands alone. Although it is unique, and quite self-explanatory, still it is vital.

When you consider being healthy, you should primarily concern yourself with developing and maintaining good habits in the areas of eating, sleeping, exercising, and physical strain. You should also be sensitive to the needs and limitations of your body and strive to maintain a balance that will not only allow you to be healthy on the day of your wedding but will also insure a long life of health and vitality. It is not surprising that when you are healthy and taking good care of your body, your mental and emotional well-being is affected as well.

My Preparedness

Goal: To evaluate how ready you are for marriage.

Evaluate how ready you are in each of the following areas. Give yourself three points if you are ready, two if you are on the way, and one if you have done nothing.

1. Social, Emotional, and Spiritual Strength
2. Literacy and Education
3. Career Development
4. Financial and Resource Management
5. Home Production and Storage
6. Physical Health

Score:

18 - Perfect	12 - Lukewarm
17 - On the way to	11 -
the celestial kingdom	10 -
16 -	9 - Cold
15 - Hot	8 -
14 -	7 -
13 -	6 - Outer darkness

Appreciation is expressed to Daniel Shade for this activity.

Are You Ready?

The first thing you ought to do is sit down with your partner and evaluate how ready you really are.

If you are ready for marriage, you can do as the scriptures say: "Have joy"! You ought to take a quiet pride and pleasure in knowing that you have arrived at a level of maturity that you are ready to enter this new and exciting stage of life. And, you can concentrate on the details of planning and getting the things done that need to be done before the wedding.

If you find that you are less ready than you thought, you have some hard decisions to make. If you aren't quite ready in a few areas, but those areas won't seriously hurt your marriage, you can still go ahead with your plans and be helpful to each other.

You may find, however, that you have some important growing up to do before you take that big and important step. You should realize that marriage is a crucial step, and if you aren't really ready, you would be so much better off to postpone your wedding or call off the engagement than to go through with it . . . and have things not work out later. The pain of breaking a marriage is much greater than that of postponing a wedding or breaking an engagement.

It may be that all you need are a few more months and a good set of plans to help you grow and mature in a few areas. You can go back over this chapter, to look at the areas in which you need more growth and sit down and make some plans about what you are going to do in the next several months to *really* be ready. Your partner will want to help you, as will your bishop and parents if you feel so inclined.

Summary

Many factors are involved in determining when a person is ready for marriage. These factors include such things as whether the person has cut the apron strings, is able to be financially independent, is emotionally mature, is old enough to marry, is objective, has a realistic conception of marriage, has a reasonable self-image, and is willing to accept responsibility for making mistakes. Even though it would seem that only Superman or Wonderwoman could have achieved perfection in these many areas before marriage, it is crucial that you consider where you are along the "perfection" ladder as you determine your personal readiness to marry.

The general idea presented is that of the importance of *acquiring skills:* This idea asserts that the number of skills a person has in behaving in the ways prescribed for a marital role influences his or her chances for marital happiness.

The six areas of personal readiness have been discussed to help you gain a perspective of just what our Heavenly Father considers crucial and timely as you prepare for an eternal relationship. Perhaps you can conclude this discussion by both completing the exercise in this chapter entitled "My Preparedness."

The thought
Of forever
Teased my mind
Like a mountain
Through a thickly
Misted view.

But today the
Veil dissolved
To show —
Eternity
Is you.
(Carol Lynn Pearson)

3

Equally Yoked?

While you are on cloud seventeen you contemplate capturing the person of your dreams. This chapter will help you examine your feelings that the person you have chosen is, in fact, the person you desire to spend eternity with. It is not intended to be a disenchanting process, but rather to cause you to look out through this cloud and make one final check to determine your suitability and "staying power" as a couple.

Paul, the ancient, in speaking to his friends in Corinth, provides a base upon which you can build: "Be ye not unequally yoked together with unbelievers: for what fellowship hath righteousness with unrighteousness? and what communion hath light with darkness? (2 Corinthians 6:14).

The bottom line here is to determine if you are "equally yoked" with your fiancé(e) so that a lasting and satisfying marriage will result.

Before continuing, you should understand that, while you have become engaged with every expectation of marrying your fiancé(e), you are not yet married. Engagement is a prelude to marriage and a season in your life when you can truly test and examine your relationship to see if an eternal chemistry exists. This should not alarm you to explore your relationship deeply, but should cause relief and security as you will then be able to marry with assurance that you haven't made an eternal mistake. You will then have used all of your resources to determine that you are truly equally yoked!

As you consider what it means to be equally yoked, consider the words of Elder Bruce R. McConkie:

> The most important things that any member of The Church of Jesus Christ of Latter-day Saints ever does in this world are . . . to marry the right person, in the right place, by the right authority. (*Mormon Doctrine*, p. 118.)

This counsel refers to marrying the right person, or in other words, marrying someone who, when sealed to oneself, forms a team that is indeed equally yoked, a team that has important things in common, and a team that pulls together.

President Spencer W. Kimball, in stressing the importance of a happy and satisfying relationship, has given a formula which, if adopted, will allow you the blessing of a celestial marriage. He indicates that this formula must be used in its entirety; that is, the principal ingredients must not be left out, reduced, or limited.

> The formula is simple; the ingredients are few, though there are many amplifications of each.
>
> *First, there must be the proper approach toward marriage, which contemplates the selection of a spouse who reaches as nearly as possible the pinnacle of perfection in all the matters that are of importance to the individuals.* Then those two parties must come to the altar in the temple realizing that they must work hard toward this successful joint living.
>
> Second, there must be great unselfishness, forgetting self and directing all of the family life and all pertaining thereunto to the good of the family, and subjugating self.
>
> Third, there must be continued courting and expressions of affection, kindness, and consideration to keep love alive and growing.
>
> Fourth, there must be complete living of the commandments of the Lord as defined in the gospel of Jesus Christ. (*Marriage and*

Divorce [Salt Lake City: Deseret Book Company, 1976], pp. 17-18;
italics added. Hereafter cited as *Marriage and Divorce*.)

As you can see, the first key to achieving a lasting and rewarding relationship is selecting as nearly as possible a mate who has
the attributes which are important to you. This you can find out
during the engagement period if not before you become engaged.
Not only does the engagement period allow you to better know
your potential spouse, but it provides an environment in which
your relationship is exposed and therefore examined. You may
both be the "cream of the marriageable crop," and yet you may
find that your relationship does not have the right chemistry to
propel you into the eternities as a couple. Becoming engaged, then,
brings changes in feelings, depth of thoughts, privileges, and expectations. With these changes come new decisions which will
further test your feelings for your fiancé(e) and your compatibility
as a couple.

Perhaps one of the biggest mistakes an engaged couple could
make would be to spend the engagement period being simply
entertained by movies, dances, and TV. You ought to make this a
time of *interaction* and exploration of your values and expectations. One of the authors counseled a young couple who had been
married two months, following a courtship of five months. During
four of these courtship months they were engaged, yet they passed
through this period being simply entertained, with almost no
interaction other than sharing physical expressions of affection
hour after degenerating hour. Following the honeymoon, they
awakened to find that neither had married the type of person he
thought he was married to. They both thought each had married
an apple. But it turned out that one partner was a peach and the
other was an orange. They are now paying the price of trying to
figure out whether they can become compatible and fulfilled in
their relationship. It's tragic to think that they didn't pay the price
of determining their compatibility prior to marriage.

How Can You Be Sure of Your Compatibility?

Just what can you do to test your relationship? Are there areas
of exploration which can enhance your possibility of experiencing

a rewarding and lasting marriage? The answer to these questions is an exciting *yes!* Consider closely several suggestions that could prove helpful in your quest.

Face Some Undesirable Situations Together

One of the most important tests a couple could use in their relationship is to face a situation in which something has to be done that neither partner wants to do. Both may be tempted to pressure the other into doing it. Such a venture may be encountered in cleaning an apartment—either their own or that of a friend. Decisions must be made such as to who will vacuum or do something equally distasteful. Or, if a couple decides to paint the house of an invalid. Who has the distasteful job of scraping and sanding? Will one scrape and the other paint, or will both share in the task? The crucial point here is that you should ask yourself how you react to each other in these types of situations. Do either of you avoid responsibility? Does one of you subtly try to coerce the other? Are you charitable or are you selfish?

> Somewhere there waiteth in this world of ours
> For one lone soul another lonely soul,
> Each choosing each through all the weary hours
> And meeting strangely at some sudden goal.
>
> When blend they like green leaves with golden flowers
> Into one beautiful and perfect whole;
> And life's long night is ended, and the way
> Lies open onward to eternal day.
> —*Edwin Arnold*

Get Away from Each Other for a While

Sometimes you can spend so much time with your fiancé(e) and your lives are so romantic that you are literally swept off your feet. You feel so much excitement and so many things are happening that you don't take the time to stop and think long and hard about your relationship. Some individuals become engaged and never again question whether they ought to marry that particular person. Therefore, one good thing to do is to get away from each other for a while. Some do this just before they are ready to announce their engagement. Others do it just prior to the wedding. Whenever you do it, it is wise to get away for a few days to clear your head, examine your relationship from afar, and weigh its strengths and weaknesses.

As you do this you may find that you are definitely ready. On the other hand, you may find that you are being too carried away with your emotions. Either way, you are better off for pausing to think clearly in a situation in which your emotions are not intense and clouded by the nearness of the relationship.

Complete the Following Questionnaire

Although these questions are not exhaustive, considering these issues together will help you know to what extent your relationship has been tried and tested.

Testing Our Engagement

Yes   No   1.   Have we visited in each other's home to the point of recognizing that normal family behavior is practiced even though the prospective in-laws are there?

Yes   No   2.   Have we become well enough acquainted with our partner's friends that we are clear about our attitudes toward them?

Yes   No   3.   Have we seen each other in a crisis or under tension or at a time when strong feelings were involved?

Yes   No   4.   Have we checked financial costs by actually looking at living quarters and shopping together and by pricing and examining furniture?

Yes   No   5.   Through open discussion, have we arrived at an understanding of how we think we should act sexually in our marriage?

Yes   No   6.   Do we agree in our expressions of affection?

Yes   No   7.   Do we enjoy being together when we are not occupied with doing something or being with other people?

Yes No 8. Have we been in situations where we had to work together as a team, such as caring for children, entertaining our families or friends, or working on a committee?

Yes No 9. Have we worked through some definite differences of opinion in a manner satisfactory to both of us?

Yes No 10. Is my fiancé(e) able and willing to accept me as I am?

Yes No 11. Am I able and willing to accept my fiancé(e) as he or she is?

Yes No 12. Have we spent a prolonged time together when each had to be his honest and unadorned self?

(Adapted from *From First Date to Chosen Mate,* by Brenton G. Yorgason. Published by Bookcraft. Copyright © 1977, by Bookcraft, Inc., pp. 120-121.)

How Similar Are You?

Perhaps you have heard that "opposites attract." Or you may have heard that "birds of a feather flock together." Which is true with regard to marriage? Is it better to be similar to or different from the other person? Or is it good to be similar in some ways and different in other ways?

There has been a great deal of research about these questions and the answer is very clear. Opposites attract in superficial relationships, and this attraction lasts for a while. A person may dream about falling in love with someone who is a prince charming or movie star, but the attraction doesn't last. It is okay to be infatuated with someone who is very different from you if it is just a temporary condition of being swept off your feet. It is *not* okay to keep the relationship going and try to build a marriage on it. Deep friendships and lasting relationships are usually with people who are *similar* to oneself. Therefore, the principle to remember is:

The more similar two people are, the better their chances of success in marriage.

This general rule is more important for some things than others. For example, being similar in height, color of hair, skin complexion, and being from the same hometown do not make any difference in marriage. Similarities in the style of life you want, your personality traits, tastes, basic values in life, expectations about marriage, philosophy of life, religion, race, aspirations, habits, and goals are much more important. And these are the things that you should discuss at great length to determine how similar you are.

You may still wonder if there aren't some areas in which it would be better to be complementary rather than similar. For example, if one person is outgoing, wouldn't it be better to marry a person who is not as outgoing? If one is a leader-type person, wouldn't that person be better off with a follower-type person? If one likes to be nurturant and take care of people, wouldn't that person be better off marrying a person who likes to be taken care of? These same questions have been asked in a number of research studies, and again the answer is that differences never seem to help. The more similar two people are, the better the marriage.

How Do You Solve Your Problems

One of the things you ought to look at carefully is how you deal with your differences and solve problems. Does one person give in all of the time? Would it be fine to keep on doing that after the marriage? Does your partner insist on getting his or her way too much, but you have hoped that that tendency would go away? Are you both considerate and thoughtful and helpful, and will that last after you are married? Do you run away from your problems or deny that you have any when you actually do have some?

Because life is full of problems and challenges, these are important questions. And after you are married, you are then left to solve most of your problems *as a couple.* It isn't that most of your problems deal with your marriage. They deal with your profession, your relatives, your health, your livelihood, your children, and your individual behavior; but it is the marital unit that usually has to deal with them. This means that you each need to develop a particular "style" of solving problems that will work for you and be comfortable for them. Usually this style starts to appear early in the relationship, and you can tell what it is long before you are married. The same style tends to remain after a couple marries — except for one typical change.

The usual change is that while courting each other you tend to be on your "best behavior." After all, you are trying to catch your partner and to improve yourself so your partner will want to marry you. The result is that *you try harder.* After you are married the typical change occurs; you will likely let up a little in how hard you try. The result is that you are usually not quite as patient, forgiving, understanding, and flexible after you marry. This pattern is not very noble, but it is at least a little understandable. What it means is that you ought to look carefully at how you solve your problems during your courtship to see if you like that style. If you do, it is one more evidence that you ought to marry your partner. If you have reservations about this area, you just have to consider it as a part of the total picture. You may still want to marry your fiancé(e), but you will be aware of an aspect of your relationship that will be less than ideal. You may think about this area and discover some serious problems in your relationship; and you may want to reconsider and examine whether you should really marry each other.

Recognize Danger Signals

As the wedding approaches, you will probably find that your relationship is either weakening or becoming stronger and more vital. Since the engagement period is a time to test the compatibility of the relationship, perhaps it would be well to discuss several danger signals which, if recognized, will help you to focus accurately on the relative strength or weakness of your relationship. As Judson Landis and Mary G. Landis point out in their book *Building a Successful Marriage* (5th ed., Englewood Cliffs, New Jersey: Prentice-Hall, 1968), in most marriages that fail, especially those that fail early, there were danger signals which, if they had been recognized by the couple, would have warned them against forming a disastrous permanent relationship. Several of these danger signals are:

The occurrence of frequent and regular lovers' quarrels. While it is true that a few quarrels may occur in potentially celestial relationships, if over a period of time quarrels continue, you should objectively evaluate what is happening. Do these quarrels have a pattern? Do certain types of events or situations tend to result in a quarrel? If you find yourself involved in a conflict-oriented relationship, your marriage will likely be this way as well.

Breaking up. It is a danger signal when you break up and make up during the engagement, especially if you do it several times. It has been found that there is a very close association between premarital confidence in the future of the relationship and later marital happiness. The patterns you begin in your dating and engagement set the stage for how you will act in your marriage, and serious instability should raise questions about whether you should remain together.

A strong desire to change the other person. A strong basic respect for your partner is very important. A desire to change your partner means a less than complete acceptance of him or her, and you would do well to remember that basic personality structure is fairly well set by the time you marry. Therefore, it is quite difficult to change oneself a great deal following marriage and almost impossible to change one's partner.

Difficulty in solving your problems. A satisfying engagement should bring out the best in both partners. For the engagement period to be characterized by feelings of depression and moodiness in one who is normally content and cheerful indicates probable danger ahead.

Avoidance. Matters that one or both of you tactfully avoid discussing or that either of you "blocks" on are the ones that should be given more serious objective thought.

Doubts. Doubts about marriage are normal. Almost all engagements are laced with doubts of one sort or another. You must remember that experiencing doubts is not important by itself. Rather, it is the *basis* for these doubts that should give you concern. You may not feel ready to marry, and so you doubt yourself. You may have doubts about your partner or even about your relationship. These doubts may be situational and could possibly be removed if something were to change. They could also be doubts which justify postponing the wedding or even terminating the engagement.

As these doubts arise, you must not camouflage or pass over them, but should consider them openly with your partner. You can test your doubts by comparing them to other big decisions you've made in life. Do you have more doubts now? And do your close associates also have doubts about your relationship? They may have some insights you don't have, and you would do well to listen to these insights. You may just be nervous, or it may be that you ought to seriously question what you are doing.

Is It Right to Call Off an Engagement?

It is sometimes justifiable to break off an engagement. If you find you are not ready for marriage or are not as compatible as you once thought, it is much better to break it off than to get married. Even though it is painful to break an engagement, it is much more painful in every way to have an unhappy marriage or to break up after you are married.

If you get in a situation in which it is wise to break the engagement, you would do well to remember that it is not a disgrace to do so. And it is best to mutually terminate a relationship so that both egos are left intact. If you must terminate the engagement without your partner's consent, you can do it tactfully. This is most easily accomplished by being critical of your relationship rather than being critical of your partner. Even though your feelings may have changed, you should keep in mind that your partner is sensitive and has feelings too; and hopefully he or she will become engaged again and marry someone else who is better suited. You can show charity by building up your partner as a person, even though you cannot continue the relationship. Nothing is accomplished by burning bridges as you leave a relationship.

Related to this frustrating situation is the question so often posed as couples struggle to free themselves from a weakening relationship: How can we break our engagement when we felt that the Lord directed us to become engaged in the first place?

This very question was asked by a friend of one of the authors. He and his partner had become engaged after a relatively short dating relationship and had done so on the basis of having received an answer to their prayers. After becoming engaged, they found themselves in the midst of many conflicts. Unable or unwilling to maintain their moral standards and realizing that they were no longer worthy to enter the temple for their marriage, they postponed the wedding date. Gradually their relationship weakened until it was finally terminated by mutual agreement.

There are several things to consider when such a serious decision seems imminent, especially when a couple feels their engagement was an answer to prayer. Many times young people feel their engagement was an answer to prayer. Many times young people are so caught up in the emotions of love that they spend but a brief moment on their knees and then arise and answer their own prayers. There is a fine line between one's emotions and the whisperings of the Spirit of the Lord. When your feelings follow a "roller coaster" pattern, up one day and down the next, they are just that — *your* feelings. But feelings from the Spirit are constant and steady, bringing to you a peace of mind and soul.

A final thought about why feelings change after someone receives an answer to prayer has to do with the reason behind the spiritual impression they received. Perhaps at certain times in our lives our Heavenly Father sees that we have a need that can be filled in a given relationship. He therefore may allow us to feel secure in this relationship for a period of time so that our particular needs can be fulfilled. This is usually not recognized by us at the time; yet in reflecting upon these meaningful relationships, we begin to realize and appreciate the wisdom of going with a particular person and planning to marry, only to later realize that we should not go through with it.

In sum, this section is included not to throw waters of doubts on your burning love but to provide a forum for you to think through the issues and implications of marrying. Now tuck these tidbits if you will in the corner of your mind as you discuss ways to make a smooth transition into marriage.

Are You Ready to Make a Commitment?

Imagine the following situation: Jane and Ron have been dating for nine months and are deeply in love. They have both dated a number of individuals and have thought long and hard about whether they should get married. Neither of them is "perfect," but they are good for each other and have a wonderful relationship. They decide to get married, and following their August wedding they move into a small apartment next to campus. As they get involved in their new ward, they develop new friendships and go out socially with several other young couples. One of their friends is Bill, who teaches the Gospel Doctrine class, and his girl friend, Sue. As they get better acquainted, Jane gradually realizes that Bill would make a much better husband for her than Ron. He is more patient, understanding, helpful, etc.

In one way or another, this same situation happens to many couples. And it is understandable. Using the husband as an example, let's say that after he is married to someone for a while, he becomes more acquainted with her faults and limitations. He learns that she, like him, is far from perfect. And as he gets to know other couples, he doesn't see all of their faults and failings (just as *he* doesn't reveal all of *his* undesirable characteristics to his friends). The result is, as the saying goes, "The grass is always greener on the other side of the fence."

There are several lessons to learn from this situation. One is that before you are really *ready* to get married, as a couple you need to be ready to make a permanent, irrevocable commitment to each other. You need to be willing to tell yourself that even though you may later meet someone else who may seem to be a better spouse, you are committed to your partner. It is the old-fashioned "for better or worse" part of marriage. Some things will turn out for the better, and you'll enjoy them; and some things will turn out for the worse, and you'll learn from them. You need to be ready to accept the undesirable aspects and live with them, not leave them and run away to a situation that seems to be better. You need to ask yourself some hard questions, such as:

> What if this person I'm about to marry develops a chronic illness, and he or she needs a lot of care and assistance? Would I still want to be married to him or her?
>
> What if I learn about some character flaws in my spouse later? Will I still stay married and love him or her?
>
> What if my spouse develops or grows in new ways that I wish he or she wouldn't? Even though this may occur, am I

ready to commit myself to this person and to the children
we will have together?
What if I meet someone who would be a better spouse for me?
Will I remain committed to my marriage, or will I leave the
marriage for the other person?

Some scholars have written about these processes, and they
have suggested that late in the courtship each person needs to
develop the opinion that "this is the best person for me that I can
get. This is the best deal for me that I know of. If I were a more
perfect person, I might be able to attract a more perfect mate; but
given my limitations, this person is the best one I can attract."
Then, after you realize that you have the best deal that you can,
you need to make a firm and unbreakable commitment to that
person and the marriage—forever.

It is only when you are truly ready to make a commitment at
this firm and irreversible level that you are truly ready for
marriage. Before that you are only ready for dating and the un-
committed, less responsible relationships that occur there. You are
not yet ready to settle down and make the firm commitments that
marriage demands. Then, after you have matured and grown,
after you realize that adult life has costs and limitations as well as
opportunities and beauty, after you are ready to commit yourself
to the other person—without reservation, for better and for
worse, forever—*then*, you are ready to marry.

Making the Transition into Marriage Easy

The change from being single to being married is perhaps the
biggest step you will ever take. You will be changing your home
and at the same time begin living with a new person. You will
change from being a single and independent person to being a
member of a partnership; and from then on decisions will be made
as a pair rather than as separate individuals. You are beginning a
relationship that will hopefully last forever. You are setting up an
entirely new household and are establishing legal obligations
toward each other. You will also begin to experience the intimacies
of sexual interaction, and you are ready to become parents. In

addition, your associates begin to treat you as a "unit" rather than as individuals.

You may find that all of these changes are exciting and rewarding, but you may also find that they are a bit overwhelming. Fortunately, researchers have learned some things that can help this transition be pleasant rather than overwhelming, exciting and fun rather than frustrating and devastating.

What have researchers discovered?

There are three main ideas that can assist you in making the transition from being single to being married. They are:

The more you learn about what is expected of you in a new role before you enter it, the easier it is to move into the role.

The more you agree in your values and role expectations, the easier it is to adjust to a new role.

The more the "social norms" (beliefs about what you ought to do) you need to comply with change when you move into a new role, the harder it is to adjust to the new role.

Perhaps we would be well to look more closely at each of these ideas as you make the transition to married life:

Prior Learning

The need for prior learning is a fairly obvious idea. If you know how to drive a car before you begin driving, it will be easier to become a good driver. If you know how to type before you get a job as a typist, it will be easier to move into the role of typist. And with marriage, the more you know about the obligations and responsibilities of marriage prior to getting married, the easier it will be to adjust to marriage. Some specific things you can do to learn what will be expected in marriage are these:

Talk with recently married couples. You will likely know couples who have been married a year or so, and you can visit with them to learn "the ropes" they have just passed through.

Avoid the mass media, or use them to learn what not to do. The scriptures teach that there is opposition in all things (2 Nephi 2:11-13), and the modern mass media are often the "opposition" in learning what is expected in marriage. Most of our modern television shows, movies, novels, and advertising distort reality so thoroughly by overromanticizing and glamorizing marriage that watching these media does more to create unrealistic expectations than to provide useful insights about marriage. Unfortunately, almost all of the media that don't paint the overly romantic point of view show just the opposite. The soap operas depict so much pathology and perverted behavior that a good rule of thumb is this: If *they* do it, *you* shouldn't do it in your life. The authors believe that the sick patterns depicted in these midday massacres constitute a subtle but devastating influence in the lives of those who watch them; when they watch them they cannot escape unscathed and uninfluenced. Many newscasts are no better. They seek for the bizarre, and sensationalize whatever they can. The result is that the mass media generally do more harm than good in teaching about marriage.

Read good books. There are a number of excellent books about marriage that can help you learn what will be expected of you in marriage. Some of them are:

Marriage and Divorce, by Spencer W. Kimball

Couples, by Carlfred Broderick

How to Have a Happy Marriage, by David and Vera Mace

Marriage Dialogue, by A. Lynn Scoresby

You and Your Marriage, by Hugh B. Brown

Marriage, Much More Than a Dream, by Rex Skidmore

Take classes. The marriage courses taught in high schools, universities, colleges, LDS institutes, and adult education centers can help you learn how you will (and how you should) behave in marriage. Some of these classes can be taken by correspondence, and the instructors are frequently so different in their approach that it may be useful to take several classes.

Agreement

There are some types of agreement that can help you adjust to marriage and others that don't matter at all. Those that do matter include agreement about basic values in life and the role expectations you have about marriage. Some areas in which agreement is irrelevant are agreement about what other couples do, how local governments should be operated, whether the Olympic Games should be subsidized by the governments, etc.

What can you do to see how much agreement you have and to create more agreement?

First of all, you can talk with each other about your expectations and about your basic values in life. In addition, you can talk with others about their expectations for their marriages, which will give you an idea about how realistic your expectations are. You should recognize that most expectations should be flexible and that partners who are flexible are those who have the most viable relationships. This is not to say that you need to vacillate in your moral convictions and other values or expectations of such magnitude, but that in the more routine parts of life flexibility is important. A final course you can take is to avoid unrealistic expectations. Sometimes couples set goals so high that they assure failure. You need to realize that everyone needs a little time to attain perfection, and some need more than a little time. We climb mountains one step at a time, and we need to progress and grow in the same way.

As you attempt to create a climate for agreement, you can perhaps complete the *Marital Inventories for LDS Couples* (the MIL). Developed by the authors of this book, the MIL is a series of questionnaires about marriage and is designed to help couples test their compatibility. The MIL is a non profit survey that contains sections that deal with how similar or different the partners are and how ready they are for marriage. The greatest value of the inventories is that they stimulate couples to discuss some topics they probably have not thought about previously. This helps them learn more about themselves and each other and to evaluate their compatibility as a couple.

The MIL is available from most instructors who teach marriage courses in LDS colleges and Institutes of Religion. If they are not readily available at these locations, they can be obtained by writing to:

MARITAL INVENTORIES FOR LDS COUPLES
Smith Family Living.Center
Brigham Young University
Provo, Utah 84602

Minimizing the Number of Norms That Change

When you marry, you will assume a large number of new obligations and responsibilities. These are "shoulds" or "oughts" that suddenly become "musts" you need to do. Some of them are simple things, such as calling your spouse on the phone when you are going to be late getting home, doing the dishes rather than letting them stack up for several days, and cutting the lawn weekly instead of annually. Other responsibilities are complicated and specified by legal or moral laws. For example, you should not commit adultery; it is immoral. Traditional laws specify that the husband has an obligation (either moral or legal) to support his wife and family. All of these things that you have to do, the little ones and the big ones, are described by the term *social norms.* Whenever you have a *large number* of social norms changing at once in your life, you will experience a difficult transition.

What are some things you can do to minimize the number of norms that change when you get married?

Timing of the marriage. If a wedding occurs at the same time that several other role transitions occur, it makes the transition into marriage more difficult. For example, if a couple were to marry, graduate from college, take a new job, move to a new city, leave their parents' homes, get called to be bishop and Relief Society president, and try to set up a small business on the side — and do all this at once — they'd have a very difficult time. They would be better off by spreading the changes out a little — and increasing their chances of survival.

Do some tasks now. The following is a list that can be considered as you attempt to minimize the changing of norms following the ceremony, to spread them out a little. While some of them may not apply to your situation, others may be practical for you:

— Combine savings accounts.
— Begin making decisions together when purchasing major items, such as furniture, insurance policies, or a car.
— Begin doing routine shopping, such as shopping for groceries, the way you will after marriage.

—Begin decision making and problem solving as you will after marriage.

—Make arrangements for any changes in residence that would ordinarily be made after you marry.

—Begin the patterns of relating to and interacting with in-laws that will exist after the wedding.

—Leave your parents' homes and "set up house" on your own or with someone else, such as a former missionary companion or friend.

Summary

This discussion about being equally yoked, while not the most enjoyable and uplifting, is one that is crucial for you as you contemplate an eternity with each other. You have become sensitive to the importance of "testing" your relationship, the legitimacy of doing so, and the methods by which to do it.

You have also learned ways to assist yourself in making a smooth and comfortable transition into marriage. Beginning your eternity together "on the right foot" is so important, and hopefully this section will help you to accomplish this end.

*When you sit with a nice girl
for two hours, you think it's
only a minute. But when you sit
on a hot stove for a minute, you
think it's two hours. That's
relativity.
(Albert Einstein.)*

4

A Preparation Timetable

"I lay in bed crying to myself as I stared at the ceiling. 'Monkey suit!' he had called it. How could he be so stubborn at such an important time? I stomped out of my bedroom, down the hall, past his room, and into the bathroom. I blew my nose as loudly as possible to make sure he knew that I was crying. Maybe if I cried loudly enough, he would hear me and know how he had hurt me!

"It was only two weeks before our wedding. Everything had been planned so carefully . . . or so I thought. I had spent hours making red aprons with white snowball fringe to complete the Christmas theme. All the red velvet dresses for the bridesmaids were completed. The tuxedos had been ordered and tried on; that is, all but my dad's! Everything was going as planned until my dad made the stubborn announcement that he had worn tuxedos at the weddings of all my older brothers and sisters and he would not be caught dead in a 'monkey suit' again.

"The next day things were no brighter. I awakened as usual and went into the kitchen where breakfast was being prepared. I made a special point not to look at my dad all during breakfast nor to speak a word to him as he drove me to work. I quickly got out of the car after arriving at work and slammed the door as hard as I dared.

"I called Craig's mother and said that I would drop in on my way home from work so that she could try on her dress. It was completed except for the white fur around the neck and sleeves.

"It had been raining. My brother and his children had consented willingly to drive me to Craig's house after work.

" 'Thanks a lot!' I said, as I started to step out of the car. Somehow one of the children grabbed my coat, causing me to lose my balance. The beautiful red velvet dress dropped into a gutter full of muddy water.

" 'I'm sorry,' Tom said.

"I tried to smile. 'Oh, that's all right,' I lied, as I stooped to pick it up. I felt like crying. It was much too late to begin making a new one, and I would never be able to get the same kind of material that had been purchased six months before. I carried the dripping, muddy dress into the house, all the time holding back a well of tears.

"As I explained what had happened, Craig's mother didn't so much as even reply, but swept the dress from my arms and headed for the washroom. As she rinsed the last of the soap from the dress and hung it near the oven, I could tell that, inspite of all my planning, I just couldn't control everything.

"Quickly days passed and with their passing came the ever-increasing realization that 'our day' was approaching all too quickly. Stopping in front of the mirror for a moment, I surveyed the blue dress I was wearing. The reflection of the bare tree branches from the window behind was a reminder that fall was over and winter would soon find me dressed in white. I imagined the long veil in the winter scene and was pleased. My smile faded with the girl in white, however, as the selfish question of the girl in blue flooded back. 'How could Craig ask me to give up the apartment this close to our wedding, and the two hundred dollars we had already paid?' My thought jumped to the conversation of the night before. Craig had called late.

" 'I know that we are not meant to move into the apartment we have rented,' he had said. I was stunned! Immediately I thought of the money. We just couldn't throw it away. He asked me to pray about it. Maybe he was right. Maybe we were supposed to live somewhere else.

"The next day we packed a card table, chairs, dishes, and food and went to the apartment. We walked through it after lunch, saying nothing. I wanted to live there so much. I stared out the bedroom window at the little pathway winding into a wooded area and knew it was perfect for us.

"As we walked into the front room Craig turned to me and said, 'Let's pray about living here.'

"We knelt down in that empty front room, and as we prayed we knew that the apartment would never be our home. We stayed for a few moments, knowing the experience we had just shared was worth far more than two hundred dollars.

"It was now just days before our wedding, and we found ourselves suddenly and desperately without an apartment, to say nothing of a place we could afford.

"Two days before our wedding the bishop of our ward completed the necessary arrangements to buy a house owned by an older lady living in a rest home. He offered the house to us as a rental unit. Before I knew what was happening, Craig had whisked me off my feet and we were heading through the front door. My tears seemed to flow without end as we gazed at the walls where paint and paper had once been placed. Even the light fixtures were bare. It didn't take long to know that the house had been unopened and uncared for for months.

"The day before our wedding was spent plastering the holes and scraping off old paint; and we even found some carpet to cover over the worn hardwood floors.

"Surprised and relieved that no further unforeseen changes had occurred, I awakened on our wedding day with a start. The excitement seemed to grow even more as we entered the temple and a worker pinned onto my dress a little card that said, 'To be married immediately.'

"We all met outside on the steps after the ceremony to take pictures. It was snowing, but somehow that didn't matter, for I had a strange and wonderful feeling of elation and joy all mixed in together. My dad held out his hand to mine and pulled me into his ever-protecting arms. He then turned to my mother and, to my surprise, said loudly enough for all to hear, 'Well, Sister B, we had better hurry if we are going to pick up the tuxedo in time!'

"A tear fell from my eye as he held me in his arms, and then off Craig and I went to prepare for the reception."

Regardless of how well prepared you become, as with this couple unforeseen problems will arise, threatening the success of your wedding day and the days that follow. Even so, you can benefit from having a timetable with which to pace the months of your engagement. While certainly not conclusive, the following timetable can be implemented to ward off that old thief of time, *procrastination.*

An Engagement Timetable

About five to six months before the wedding
- Counsel with both parents about the wedding. Honor them first (Exodus 20:12).
- Discuss degree of formality and size of reception.
- Discuss the budget with parents. (If you're going to share expense, be sure to include both sets of parents.)
- Choose the temple to be married in.
- Decide how many guests. Let both parents know how many they may invite and when the lists of names need to be ready.
- Reserve the place for the reception, wedding breakfast, etc.
- Select engagement ring.
- Discuss ideas for your new home with your fiancé(e). Begin at least window shopping.

About four months before the wedding
- Select patterns for china, crystal, silver, linens; and register preferences with favorite store's bridal gift registry.

—Decide color scheme and let mothers know so they can begin arranging for their dresses.
—Choose attendants.
—Choose and order their dresses and accessories.
—Plan a trousseau. Begin to shop.
—Make arrangements with photographer.
—Plan menu. Arrange catering. Find out if cake is included in catering.

About three months before the wedding

—Have interviews with bishops or branch presidents and then with stake presidents. Ask yourself the following questions (similar ones may be part of the interview):

1. Am I worthy and ready to enter the temple?
2. What is the procedure if we are not ready?
3. If I have a current recommend, do I need another one for the marriage ceremony?
4. Have the bishop and I included all the vital information required on the recommend?
5. Have I been completely honest in answering questions?
6. Have I been a member of the Church at least 365 days?
7. Have I cleared any previous divorce actions?
8. Have I invited and welcomed counsel from the bishop, and am I prepared to follow it?

—Order invitations. Have the envelopes sent right away so you can begin addressing them.
—Order personal stationery or thank-you notes.
—Choose and order wedding dress and accessories; or if you are making it, don't delay beginning this project another day!
—Select type of wedding cake and order it.
—Make appointment with family doctor or gynecologist for physical exam and blood test. If planning a honeymoon abroad, allow time for inoculations.
—Order bride's books.
—Make reservations for any clothing that will be rented, such as tuxes for the men.

About two months before the wedding

—Decide the schedule for the wedding day. Schedule the time

to be sealed, the time for a wedding breakfast, etc. Be sure to leave the day relatively uncluttered. It is a big day that should be a time of great joy, not of frantically rushing around from one thing to another.

—Discuss all of the details of your reception with the people in charge: caterer, musicians, manager at the reception center, etc.

—Make final arrangements for special aspects of reception, such as flowers, music, photos, canopies, carpets, lights, etc.

—Choose and order gifts for attendants.

A month or so before the wedding

—*Call, write, or personally visit the marriage desk clerk in the temple of your choice.* Use complete, correct, current information received directly from the clerk and base your marriage plans on this information. Hearsay or even information from well-meaning friends and relatives or temple goers may cause you grief. The clerk may answer the following questions:

1. Are our recommends in order? Does the temple need additional data?
2. Can we set a marriage day and hour for the wedding in advance so that we may plan in accordance with our needs?
3. What must we do to procure a marriage license acceptable to the specific temple in which we are getting married?
4. What kind of blood test is acceptable?
5. Is there a waiting period after the issuance of the marriage license? How late can the license be used?
6. Are there different marriage arrangements, one of which we may choose in accordance with our personal marriage situation?
7. Which arrangement is recommended for us?
8. Who selects the witnesses and sees that they are present?
9. Who will perform the sealing ceremony? May we talk with this official ahead of time?

10. How many guests may we invite, and what are the essential instructions we must give them?
11. How long does the entire marriage procedure generally last?
12. What day and hours seem the least busy in the temple?
13. May the mother of the bride accompany her?
14. What courtesies are available for nonmember or non-recommend-holding parents?
15. What instructions would we receive about our clothing needs?
16. What do we need to know about parking, picture taking, music, rice throwing, etc.?
17. What can we do to make our marriage day a reverent and sacred experience?

— Mail invitations.
— Order wedding cake if it is not included in the catering.
— Have final fitting of wedding dress and accessories.
— Arrange lodging for out-of-town attendants and relatives.
— Choose wedding present for mate if you are to exchange gifts — it's optional
— Both have thorough physical examinations. Obtain blood tests if the state law requires them.
— Make appointments for permanents and hairstyling.
— Attend showers.
— Have wedding portrait taken.
— Prepare newspaper announcement.
— Arrange transportation for guests and relatives if necessary.
— Make arrangements for a place to keep gifts as they arrive.
— Make arrangements for packing and moving if it is necessary.
— Make reservations for motels, etc., for honeymoon.

Several weeks before the wedding
— Record gifts that are received.
— Take announcement to newspaper.
— Make check with caterer, reception facilities, etc.
— Get marriage license.
— Complete trousseau shopping. Make sure items will be delivered on time.

— Wrap gifts for attendants.
— Arrange to change names and addresses on bank and shared accounts, personnel records, social security, insurance or health policies, driver's license, etc.
— Send thank-you notes to those who may have attended a shower for you.

A week or so before the wedding
— Give or go to bridesmaid's luncheon or party if desired.
— Give final guest estimate to caterer.
— Begin packing for honeymoon.
— Begin moving into your new apartment.
— Keep up those thank-you notes.

The day of the wedding
— Relax and enjoy every moment of it.
— Remember to take marriage license, temple recommends, cameras, etc.

Who Does What?

Tradition has created many conventions about weddings; and responsibilities can be divided according to these traditions. You should, however, feel free to adapt them to your individual circumstances. The traditional division of responsibilities is as follows:

Bride's responsibilities:
— Getting her temple recommend.
— Selecting attendants.
— Purchasing the groom's wedding ring.
— Helping her parents in making arrangements for parties, receptions, etc.
— Getting her wedding dress.
— Getting her trousseau.
— Selecting colors and theme for reception.
— Purchasing presents for bridesmaids.
— Getting personal stationery.
— Getting medical exam.
— Assuming some of parents' duties.

Groom's responsibilities:
— Getting his temple recommend.

— Purchasing the bride's wedding rings.
— Choosing best man and ushers.
— Buying gifts for best man, ushers, and bride.
— Getting marriage license.
— Getting bride's bouquet.
— Getting wedding certificate.
— Getting mothers' flowers.
— Getting medical exam.
— Buying boutonnieres for men.
— Providing accommodations for best man and ushers.

Couple's responsibilities:
— Deciding what to do for the honeymoon.
— Meeting with bishops or branch presidents and stake presidents.
— Sending thank-you notes.

Bride's parents' responsibilities:
— Sending invitations.
— Sending announcements.
— Arranging for photographs.
— Arranging the rental of reception hall.
— Paying fees for music.
— Getting flowers for reception.
— Getting bridesmaids' bouquets.
— Planning transportation.
— Arranging bridesmaids' luncheon.
— Preparing for refreshments at reception.
— Getting wedding gift.
— Arranging for wedding cake.

Groom's parents' responsibilities:
— Clothes for ushers.
— Own traveling expenses.
— Wedding gift.
— Wedding breakfast.
— Call on bride's family.
— Express approval.
— Guest list for reception.

Best man's responsibilities:
— Be in charge of ushers.

— Bring wedding ring to ceremony.
— Help groom prepare for wedding.
— Stand in wedding reception line next to groom.
— Assist couple in getting away from reception.

Ushers' responsibilities:
— Receive gifts at door of reception center.
— Assist at reception (coat removal, etc.).
— Head usher assists wedding party and photographer, stands at head of wedding line.

Summary

While this section has been somewhat unique, still it has served the purpose of making you aware of the multitude of tasks which must be performed by everyone involved with the wedding. In addition, you have hopefully now defused your expectations of everything happening "without a hitch," as last-minute changes and interruptions are inevitable.

It would now be appropriate for you to shift mental gears and take a much different course as you consider your physical relationship and just what is involved in being man and wife.

The timetable and list of responsibilities on these pages are adapted from several lists developed by others. Elmer Knowles and Harold Glen Clark at Brigham Young University have prepared lists that are appropriate for LDS couples, and their ideas are summarized here. Appreciation is expressed to them for permission to use and to reproduce their ideas. Also, some ideas were gleaned from *Brides Magazine Wedding Planner*, and appreciation is expressed to that source.

Therefore shall a man leave **5**
his father and mother, and shall
cleave unto his wife: and they
shall be one flesh.
(Genesis 2:24.)

Intimacy in an Eternal Perspective

As you approach the wedding day you will likely find yourself increasingly aware of the changes that are going to take place in your relationship with your partner as you become *one flesh.* Whereas prior to marriage you tuck this aspect of your relationship quietly and safely away on a shelf, your wedding day will find you anxiously unwrapping this dimension of marriage. For some young Latter-day Saints this is a beautiful and sacred dimension, but for others it becomes the unsettled foundation upon which an unpleasant and unsatisfying physical relationship is established. The purpose of this discussion is to prepare you, as prospective bride and groom, to develop a mutually rewarding and fulfilling physical environment in which warmth and trust and acceptance can flourish.

As you approach this topic, you ought to do so with reverence. You should not have fear, and you should not treat it in a hush-hush manner between your two selves. Sexual expression in marriage is not a taboo topic and it is not secret. But *it is a sacred topic.* This means that you should treat it in a revered and special way.

Why Should You Discuss Married Intimacy Now?

While other reasons may exist, it appears that there are four primary reasons or justifications for discussing marital intimacy as you approach the threshold of married life. These are as follows:

First: You are being bombarded with misinformation about sex which needs to be corrected.

Our society is passing through a unique historical period. During the Puritan and Victorian periods, it almost seems as if the existence of sex was often denied, and certainly some inappropriately repressive views about it were common. For example, the view prevailed that sexual intercourse is a necessary evil that should simply be "tolerated," and that it is the man's right and the woman's duty. The twentieth century has experienced a reaction against these excessive views. Unfortunately, this reaction has done more than just correct the errors of the past. Like a pendulum swinging too far, we have moved into a period of excessive permissiveness, where sex is flaunted and portrayed and abused. It is crucial that LDS couples stand fast and firm rather than allow themselves to be tossed to and fro with every wind of worldly beliefs and practices. We need to avoid the extreme views of the Puritan and Victorian eras, but we need to avoid also the hedonistic extremes of our own sexually "liberated" times. To do this we need to identify an eternal perspective on sexuality.

Second: Seek after that which is lovely and praiseworthy.

The thirteenth article of faith states that members should seek after that which is "virtuous, lovely, or of good report or praiseworthy." This is true in the sexual area as much as any other part of life. Biological, medical, and social scientists have been discovering new information in many different areas of life, and just as these discoveries are welcomed when they deal with farming skills, management processes, technology, and so on, so we should receive them when they deal with the sexual part of life. You need to follow this article of faith, to look to the sciences for additional information about sexuality too, and then use that information *whenever it is consistent with the revealed truths.*

Third: Avoid apostate beliefs concerning sexuality.

There are members of the Church who have naively accepted the belief that the physical part of the body is evil and debasing and should be shunned and avoided. This belief dates back to ancient philosophies, and it continues to exist in several modern cultures. It springs from the concept that the mind or the spirit is the more pure or righteous part of man, and the physical body is the seat of evil things such as passions and corrupting influences. This concept led its advocates to seek enhancement of the mental or spiritual parts while avoiding physical pleasures. From this it was a short step to defining the sexual part of man as primarily a part of the physical body rather than of the spirit, thereby labeling sexuality as evil, carnal and undesirable. This belief was incorporated into early apostate Christian traditions and has unfortunately crept into the minds and hearts of some Latter-day Saints as well.

The debasing view that the physical body is something low and that sexuality in marriage is unholy or evil is incompatible with revealed truths about the nature of man. The restored gospel teaches that each of us is a temple (1 Corinthians 3:16-17), and that, since the physical body was made in the image of God, it is glorious and desirable. We are born innocent and pure. Then, as we grow up, we learn to do wrong and thereby become fallen. But evils in us are not confined to the physical body. They arise in the heart and mind and spirit, and then our bodies may become victims of our unrighteousness rather than the source of it. In its mortal state, the physical body is subject to a variety of frailties and imperfections, but normal sexual drives and feelings are not in that category. The Lord gave us sexuality and commanded us to use it for His eternal purposes—and He called His work good (Genesis 1:31). Can we do any less? The Lord has cautioned us against viewing good things as evil: ". . . do not judge that which is evil to be of God, or that which is good and of God to be of the devil" (Moroni 7:14).

Fourth: The sexual part of marriage is a crucial part.

A final reason you should deal with sexuality openly is that it is not a trivial area which you can ignore. It is a very important part of marriage. As Elder Hugh B. Brown has written:

> Many marriages have been wrecked on the dangerous rocks of ignorant and debased sex behavior, both before and after marriage. Gross ignorance on the part of newlyweds on the subject of the proper place and functioning of sex results in much unhappiness and many broken homes. (*You and Your Marriage* [Salt Lake City: Bookcraft, 1960], p. 73.)

Most people agree that it is important to learn about money management, how to get along with in-laws, child rearing, affection, and tenderness, because these are important areas of marriage. They agree that if they are inept or unskillful in these areas it will disrupt the marriage relationship. Is it any less so in the sexual area? Many people do not learn about the sexual aspect of life from their parents or peers. Many Church members are converts who grew up in undesirable settings and learned many unwholesome beliefs and practices about sexuality. In addition, everyone is exposed to horrible practices in the mass media in which the man is to be the aggressor and the woman pursued, and the woman is to be sought for the gratification of the man. Almost all TV and movie scripts teach that seduction, hiding information about genuine feelings, exploitation, and partial truths are the best way to have physically intimate interaction. They also teach that all that is needed in marriage is for the man and woman to "be in love"; if they are in love, everything will turn out all right. These beliefs are so inaccurate, so unwise, in some cases so heinous, that it is no wonder the divorce rate has been skyrocketing.

As a soon-to-be bride or groom, then, you should deal with the sexual part of marriage openly because that part makes so much difference in marriage, and because there is so much misinformation or lack of information about how to interact wisely and effectively. You must learn to deal with this part carefully, tactfully, tastefully, and reverently, and you must do it in ways that are consistent with revealed truths, *but you must do it* if you are to be a wise steward over this part of your life.

An Eternal Perspective on Physical Intimacy

With your understanding of the importance of knowing about and being sensitive to this sacred part of marriage, you should begin your quest for an eternal perspective on it. This discussion should properly start at the "beginning."

When your spirit body was organized in your premortal life, it was created according to natural laws by your being born to heavenly parents. As a spirit child you lived with these parents and were tutored by them. You recognized the differences between their glorified, immortal bodies and your limited spirit body, and you eagerly anticipated the day when you would be like them and possess the powers which were theirs. You were taught it would be necessary to leave your pleasant premortal surroundings — that you needed to be tried and tested and to grow by facing adversities before you would be worthy of your heavenly parents' procreative powers. This process of living on an earth to prove one's worthiness and grow in worthiness is part of the plan of salvation, a plan designed to assist you in achieving your full potential by becoming like your heavenly parents.

There are many concepts in the plan of salvation. Three of them are as follows:

1. Men and women are to come to the earth and receive mortal, temporal bodies. While upon this earth, they are to have *free agency* in their actions, in how they use these bodies. That is, they are stewards over their own behavior, and as such they will be held accountable for their actions and the way they use their bodies.
2. Through a proper use of this agency each is to prepare himself for an eternal companion and select that companion, in the process creating an eternal unit.
3. With that companion, and under the direction of the Holy Spirit, each is to participate in one of the most sacred experiences possible — that of procreation. This process per-

mits spirits to come to the earth in physical bodies to experience their turn in mortality.

These procreative powers are central to the plan. It is the proper use of these powers within the marriage covenant that makes it possible to have that which our heavenly parents have — an eternal family. The wise use of these powers in this life will make it possible for you to retain the reproductive powers and have them extended and expanded throughout the eternities. (D&C 131:4; 132:15-20.)

As Elder Boyd K. Packer has stated, the power of procreation is in fact the *very key* to happiness, being central to the entire plan of salvation. It is the way provided for our spirit brothers and sisters to enter this life and thus prepare for an eternal life with a companion and with our Father in Heaven.

As Elder Packer has also pointed out, this creative power that lies within each of us exhibits two significant features; it is both *strong* and *constant.* Knowing the difficulties encountered in rearing children, our Heavenly Father provided these features to motivate us to bring His children to the earth, since without these features many would be reluctant to accept the awesome responsibilities of parenthood.

The Lord also understood the elements of opposition facing His children in marriage, so He also made this experience a bonding and unifying one for both men and women. By this we understand that this power was to be constant, to allow couples a medium for developing, expressing, and fostering delicate and intimate love feelings. Contrary to much that is in modern literature, the experience of procreation is not a self-oriented, personal gratification experience; within marriage it becomes one in which feelings of love, caring, and giving expand and grow. When two people have this understanding, they experience the highest and most noble feelings of love and companionship. Then and only then can two really become one and share in the depth of purpose of this experience — that is, to participate with our Heavenly Father in literally creating a body.

Our Desires Are Inherently Good

Several man-made philosophies teach that the sexual aspects of man and woman are evil—that they are carnal and sensual and devilish. This view is an unfortunate and pernicious belief that distorts one of the most beautiful aspects of life. In the April 1974 General Conference, President Spencer W. Kimball quoted Billy Graham as follows:

> "The Bible makes plain that evil, when related to sex means not the use of something inherently corrupt but the *mi*suse of something pure and good. It teaches clearly that sex can be a wonderful servant but a terrible master: that it can be a creative force more powerful than any other in the fostering of a love, companionship, happiness or can be the most destructive of all of life's forces." ("Guidelines to Carry Forth the Work of God in Cleanliness," *Ensign*, May 1974, pp. 7-8. Hereafter referred to as "Guidelines.")

In sum, it is important to remember that this sacred power of procreation is the very key to exaltation in the celestial kingdom. It is a sobering thought that only those who prepare for and then build an eternal relationship can participate in this sacred, life-creating act throughout the eternities, as exalted *couples*—the only marriage partners to continue as husband and wife, father and mother, forever.

The Purposes of the Sexual Part of Marriage

There is a segment of the Christian world which believes that the sexual part of marriage is only for the purpose of procreation. According to this belief, couples should engage in intercourse only when their motive is to conceive. This idea differs markedly from a second view about the purposes of sex, which is that the sexual part of marriage has two major functions—*procreation* as well as *enhancement of the husband-wife relationship*. This difference is important because it leads to very different behavior in marriage. Those who believe that there are two purposes feel that sexual intercourse is desirable when couples have motives such as the expression of love, closeness, relaxation, making up, and tenderness. Those who believe that procreation is the only function of sex would not engage in intercourse at these times. They would also not have intercourse during pregnancy or at any other time when conception is not desired.

This issue is a sensitive one in the LDS community because some have publicly advocated one position and others have advocated the other. Apparently the Lord has not spoken on the matter, and so it is an issue regarding which differences of opinion are understandable. The authors think the belief that sex is only for procreation originated in the apostate concept that was discussed earlier (the idea that the body is evil while the mind and spirit are pure). This view was incorporated into Christian theology after the Apostasy and found its way into the thinking of some early Latter-day Saints because it was an assumed part of their culture before they were converted.

Expressions of some earlier Church leaders suggest that they viewed sexual expression as having the two functions of procreation and enhancing the marriage relationship. Elder Parley P. Pratt, in his *Key to the Science of Theology* stated:

> The object of the union of the sexes is the propagation of their species, or procreation; also for mutual affection and the cultivation of those eternal principles of never-ending charity and benevolence which are inspired by the Eternal Spirit; also for mutual comfort and assistance in this world of toil and sorrow and for mutual duties toward their offspring. (1855, p. 173.)

Similarly, President Joseph F. Smith wrote:

> The lawful association of the sexes is ordained of God, not only as the sole means of race perpetuation, but for the development of the higher faculties and nobler traits of human nature, which the love-inspired companionship of man and woman alone can insure. ("Unchastity the Dominant Evil of the Age," *Improvement Era*, Vol. 20, 1917, p. 739.)

President Spencer W. Kimball likewise has addressed this issue. In the April 1974 General Conference, he quoted with approval the following statement from Billy Graham:

> ". . . The Bible celebrates sex and its proper use, presenting it as God-created, God-ordained, God-blessed. It makes plain that God himself implanted the physical magnetism between the sexes for two reasons: for the propagation of the human race, and for the expression of that kind of love between man and wife that makes for true oneness. His command to the first man and woman to be 'one flesh' was as important as his command to 'be fruitful and multiply.' " ("Guidelines," p. 7.)

Again, in 1975, President Kimball stated:

> We know of no directive from the Lord that proper sexual experience between husbands and wives need be limited totally to the procreation of children, but we find much evidence from Adam until now that no provision was ever made by the Lord for indiscriminate sex. ("The Lord's Plan for Men and Women," *Ensign*, Oct. 1975, p. 4.)

Thus it is suggested that the sexual part of man and woman was created for wise and noble reasons, to reproduce as well as to unite, uplift, exalt, and glorify.

Summary

The purpose of this discussion has been to allow you to see, as one might view a beautiful forest, the magnitude of the blessing of marital intimacy as created by our Heavenly Father. It now becomes appropriate and timely to focus on and examine the individual timbers that make up the forest fiber. As you do, it is hoped that you will take advantage of your spiritual binoculars, so that what you learn will be spiritually internalized (rather than exploited) as you continue to prepare for your marriage union.

All true love is grounded on a sensitive trust, a complete respect, and a concern for the mate which is in all respects equal to the concern for self. (Brenton G. Yorgason.)

6

Appropriate Responding in Intimacy

Our Heavenly Father has indicated that to Him all things are spiritual (D&C 29:34). This includes the sexual part of marriage. The physical union of a husband and wife can be a moment when they are partners with God in the creation of new life. It is the process which helps the Lord complete His plan by bringing His spirit children to their earthly existence.

Proper sexual interaction is also spiritual in the sense that it helps two people draw closer to each other in trust and affection. It is the most intimate type of giving and sharing, and it helps build bonds that can last forever. When used properly, it can also bring a couple closer to the Holy Spirit and expand their spiritual qualities. As Parley P. Pratt has written:

> The gift of the Holy Ghost adapts itself to all these organs or attributes [that man has which are possessed by God Himself]. It

quickens all the intellectual facilities, increases, enlarges, expands
and purifies all the natural passions and affections; and adapts them,
by the gift of wisdom to their lawful use. (Parley P. Pratt, *Key to
Theology,* 1883, p. 101.)

Physical and Emotional Dimensions of Intimacy

While our discussion to this point has been centered around the
eternal perspective of intimacy in marriage, it now becomes
appropriate to move much closer to this part of marriage. As you
proceed, you will find that this discussion deals with the specific
moments of intimacy. It is not intended that this be a departure
from the foundation already provided, but rather a close exami-
nation of this important area which must be carefully and sensitively placed upon that foundation. As you learn of the physical
and emotional dimensions of intimacy, keep in mind that the
mortar used in this part of marriage, as in the other areas of
married life, consists of the Holy Ghost. It is hoped that as you
now look into the more specific issues, you will do so with
spiritual eyes, with a desire to learn of the sexual experience in such
a way that your marriage will begin in a positive environment
rather than in one fraught with fears, mistrust, and misconceptions. Attune yourself now to the Spirit as together you look
more deeply yet sensitively into the experience of the physical
union of husband and wife.

The Cycle in Physical Intimacy

One of the insights gained about physical intimacy is that there
is a cycle in the way a man and woman become sexually fulfilled.
This cycle has four different stages, and each person experiences
physiological, psychological, and emotional changes in each stage.
The four stages are:
— The Excitement Stage
— The Plateau Stage
— The Orgasm Stage
— The Resolution Stage
The excitement phase. Most of the time we are not experi-
encing sexual feelings. Our minds are occupied with other things,

such as studying, working, eating, cleaning our home, doing our Church work, etc. But every once in a while something happens that creates a slight sexual feeling. We may be holding hands at a special moment, or we may touch each other in just the right way, or our eyes may meet in a special glance. There are many circumstances that can create these initial feelings of intimate attraction.

Like any other emotion, sexual excitement begins as a very small feeling. Also, like any other emotion, this feeling can grow and expand until it becomes intense. While we cautiously guard ourselves in dating relationships from allowing these feelings to become intense and dominate our relationship inappropriately, when we are married these feelings are natural and healthy in our relationship. In addition, having intense feelings in marriage is good because when we are mentally and emotionally "swept away" by our feelings, this excitement creates a number of changes in both the husband's and the wife's body that help prepare for the sexual union.

This complex process of the mind, the emotions, and the anatomy all working together to prepare a couple for the act of love is beautiful, and it helps explain why the Lord created our bodies with these "strong" and "constant" drives and emotions. There are those who miss the extreme feelings of sexual fulfillment, beginning and completing the act as quickly as possible. These couples fail to recognize that the Lord placed the emotional and mental responses in them, and that these responses make the reproductive process more effective, natural, and enjoyable. The extensive loving and caressing that assist in creating the sexual excitement actually help prepare the bodies for the later stages of the sexual cycle.

The plateau phase. There is a plateau in the process of moving from the state of no sexual excitement to the most intense feelings. The participants usually experience more and more excitement gradually until they reach the plateau, when both the husband's and the wife's mental concerns are primarily with this intimate expression, and they experience a continual feeling of fairly intense elation and enjoyment.

There is an important difference in the way the husband and the wife usually responds in the excitement and plateau phases. The husband usually moves through the excitement phase more quickly than the wife. When this occurs he is physiologically and emotionally ready to participate in the sexual act before she is. If the couple tries to complete the sexual union at that time, it can create several problems. The wife may not be physiologically ready, so at that time the act can be uncomfortable or even painful for her. She may not be emotionally ready and may therefore resent the husband's attempts to effect the union. If this pattern is repeated frequently and over a long period of time, it can build mutual resentment and frustration regarding the entire sexual part of marriage.

It is therefore important for you as a married couple to gradually learn how to love each other in ways that allow you both to move through the natural cycle of becoming aroused and excited, so that your bodies are prepared for the mating act. You need to take the time to love and caress each other rather than rush into the experience. Most couples enjoy this normally, though at some times with some couples they find it pleasant to have shorter love-making sessions. You will find that each of you have your own unique interests and abilities and apprehensions; and you ought to use the first months of your marriage as a time to learn how to respond to each other and how to love in a way that will be mutually pleasant and fulfilling.

The plateau phase can last a short time or a long time, depending on the desires of the couple. If they want to reach the sexual climax quickly, they can stimulate each other until they achieve fulfillment. Some couples who remain in this phase for several hours find that mildly uncomfortable feelings, much like a mild cramp, develop in the lower abdomen. Unmarried couples who have a relationship that is inappropriately centered around heavy physical involvement, and yet who wish to remain "technically chaste" by not going all the way, sometimes conclude a romantic session with these uncomfortable feelings or cramps. These couples are merely teasing their emotions and their bodies by preparing for full intimacy while wanting to remain virtuous prior to marriage. Perhaps this is another of the reasons why Church leaders have counseled young couples against "making out" sessions prior to marriage.

The orgasmic phase. This is usually the shortest of the four phases, as it seldom lasts more than a few seconds. It is the brief period when the climax or peak of sexual excitement occurs. This climax has three components in the husband: (a) semi-involuntary muscular contractions in the entire abdominal area, (b) an extremely intense and pleasant sensation, and (c) an ejaculation of semen, which contains life-producing chromosomes. The ejaculation is only about a half-teaspoon in volume, but it contains up to 500,000 sperm.

The climax for the wife has two components: (a) a series of semi-involuntary muscular contractions, similar to the husband's and (b) the same type of intense and pleasant sensations. The wife's body does not experience anything comparable to the male ejaculation.

The resolution phase. The final phase of the sexual embrace is a period of gradual reduction in sexual excitement. The resolution in the male is involuntary and begins to occur within a few seconds after the ejaculation. The entire resolution phase for him may be over in a period as short as ten to thirty seconds. He then enters a period of sexual satiation, as his physiological and psychological ability to respond to restimulation is low for a period of time. As men grow older they find that this satiation or refractory period gradually increases as their bodies require longer periods of time to recuperate.

The wife usually moves through the resolution phase much more slowly than the husband, as she frequently experiences a period known as the "after-glow." What this means is that her interest in being physically close and romantic may take fifteen to thirty minutes to gradually subside. It is important that couples understand this natural difference between the husband and wife, because if it is ignored it can cause resentments. The husband may be inclined to "roll over and go to sleep," but he needs to learn how to continue to meet his wife's needs. He can at least be a pleasant conversationalist, and can also learn to enjoy being close and romantic, empathetic and understanding, during this time. The wife too needs to understand about the fact that his interest in sexual interaction has probably subsided more rapidly than hers. It is interesting as well to note that, unlike the husband, the wife has no satiation or refractory period following orgasm.

Emotions Influence What Happens

Sexual interaction is so delicate and sensitive that it is easily influenced by other emotions. When a couple has a relationship in which peace, harmony, unity and trust prevail, this helps the sexual interaction. It creates an atmosphere of trust and acceptance wherein they want to be close to each other and express their feelings of love and tenderness. On the other hand, if a couple has unresolved disagreements that are bothering them, or if they feel resentment or animosity, these feelings interfere with the sensitive feelings they need for pleasant sexual interaction and fulfillment.

The sexual part of a marriage is therefore a good barometer of how well things are going in a relationship. If the sexual part of the marriage is going well, then other parts are probably also going well. If a couple is having problems with the sexual part of their lives, it is likely that some of the other areas are also having problems. More often than not, the sexual problems are not at the root of their difficulties. Their sex life is the victim of the problems in the other areas.

Anxiety. There are two kinds of negative emotions that are particularly disruptive. One of these consists of anxiety about the sexual part of marriage. When growing up, some people gained the impression that sexual intimacy was dirty or evil, or that sex was something to be endured rather than enjoyed. These beliefs tend to create anxiety as a person matures and begins to anticipate the sexual dimension of marriage. He or she feels tense, nervous, uncomfortable, and ill at ease, and these feelings interfere with the spontaneity and freedom needed to achieve complete satisfaction and fulfillment.

These feelings of anxiety can sometimes be very disruptive for the wife. If she is anxious, the anxiety tends to make her tighten up inside. This keeps the muscles and tissues in the abdominal and pelvic area from relaxing in a normal way as she enters the excitement phase of the sexual response cycle. When this occurs, it makes the sexual experience difficult and uncomfortable.

What are some solutions if you have this problem?

First, you need to develop a healthy, positive attitude toward the sexual part of marriage. If you have considered it dirty, evil, and unpleasant, or if you are not looking forward to it for some other reason, you need to get some help and change your opinion *and* your feeling. You can discuss your feelings with your fiancé(e) just before you are married. If your parents would be helpful, you can talk to them. Sometimes, however, you may have learned undesirable beliefs from your parents, and their counsel on this therefore would not be helpful. You may want to talk to your bishop about your feelings, since these uncomfortable feelings are sometimes associated with guilt and feelings of inappropriateness about your thoughts, desires, or behavior. You can also obtain medical assistance if necessary, or see a counselor who has been trained in this area (preferably a Church member or one with similar views on this topic).

A second thing you can do to cope with your feelings of anxiety is to realize that most couples have these same anxieties in the first few weeks and months of marriage. They are taught as they grow up to be modest and clothed around members of the opposite sex. Then, after a short ceremony, they can be open and spontaneous sexually. They are commanded to multiply and replenish the earth, and they are expected to begin to have an active sex life. This is a dramatic change, and most persons experience some anxiety as they first begin this part of marriage. They are not used to being around someone of the opposite sex in such an intimate way, and they are not sure how to act. These feelings are normal, and if you find yourself experiencing them, the following suggestions can help you overcome them.

1. This is a time in your relationship when you need to be unusually patient and considerate of the other person's wishes and feelings. You need to listen to what the other person says about his feelings *and believe them,* and respond accordingly. If your partner wants to stop and wait, respect those wishes *and* the feelings that are behind the wishes. You have waited for years to begin interacting in this way, and you should be willing, if necessary, to control yourself and wait a little longer.

2. You need to move into the sexual part of your marriage

slowly. This means that neither person should force himself on the other. Instead, you ought to go only as fast as the slowest individual wants to go. Let the one who is the most reluctant determine the pace. One of you may not want to have intercourse the first day or night. A few hours or days of patience at this stage of your marriage may create an environment of trust and acceptance and understanding that will be invaluable over the years.

3. You need to remember that in the sexual response cycle, the female is only fully ready physiologically to participate in intercourse after she has experienced enough of the excitement phase that the pelvic area has relaxed. Therefore, you may find it useful to have at least a moderate amount of loving before beginning intercourse.

4. Talk, talk, talk, talk. . . . Then talk some more! You can only understand how each other feels, what each wants, what each is anxious about, and what each doesn't want, by verbalizing to the other person. Nonverbal communication skills don't take us very far initially in this area of marriage, and it is very easy to misinterpret nonverbal messages. Therefore, talk about what you are experiencing, what you enjoy or don't enjoy, what excites, what is undesirable, etc.

Negative feelings. A second type of emotion that has a large effect on the sexual part of marriage is negative feelings toward the other person. Whenever a person has negative feelings such as resentment, anger, fear, distrust, animosity, and hurt, these feelings interfere with the sexual part of marriage. This seems to be the case more for wives than husbands, but it occurs for both.

Everyone has problems, and every husband and wife will at times have negative feelings toward each other. If they resolve these problems and feelings so they don't carry them around for long periods of time they will not interfere with a couple's normal desire to be close physically for brief moments — and then they can "make up." When couples do not resolve the basic problems in their relationship, when they carry their negative feelings around for long periods of time, just as surely as night follows day it will eat away like an acid at the sexual part of their marriage (and at other parts too).

Increasing Your Effectiveness

As you prepare for marriage and for the experience of being a "couple" rather than simply an individual, there are many things you can do to increase your effectiveness in the sexual part of marriage. Several keys to being effective are to be loving, get involved, talk extensively, create security, enjoy physical contact with each other, and seek help when you need it.

Be Loving

It is likely that loving behaviors influence a couple's sexual interaction as much as any area, and maybe more. As you interact sexually, you need to remember to be patient, kind, and understanding. You need to avoid being puffed up and only caring about yourself. The Lord's admonitions about gentleness, compassion, tenderness, mercy, thoughtfulness, forgiveness, and concern for others ought to be the hallmark of our thoughts and feelings and actions at all times, and are especially important in sexual interaction. And, on the other hand, the ways of behaving that the Savior opposes so continually are especially inappropriate in the intimate interaction between a husband and wife. Therefore, force, coercion, lack of consideration, arrogance, unrighteous dominion, deception, exploitation, half-truths, and selfishness ought to be expelled completely from the bedroom as well as from the rest of the house.

Become Involved

Medical researchers have discovered that some individuals are sexually ineffective because they tend to be "spectators" as they participate in sex. They remain a little aloof — they observe what is happening around them rather than becoming totally involved in the experience. One thing that can cause this is spending too much time thinking and reading about sexual techniques. Apparently too much academic involvement, like too little understanding, can be harmful.

As the response cycle indicates, this intellectual analyzing is an unnatural way to behave because the natural thing is to gradually become totally immersed in the sexual experience and forget about other things. If you find that the sexual part of your marriage is not what you think it should be, you may want to examine whether you are remaining a spectator by not getting fully involved emotionally.

There are a number of things you can do to promote total involvement. You can put a lock on your bedroom door so you will feel comfortable with total privacy; you can arrange the drapes in your room so you will have complete privacy; and you can have an apartment or house that will give you complete isolation. You can also allow enough time in your busy lives for the sexual part of life. The sexual feelings in most individuals cannot be turned on and off in a few minutes, and couples need considerable time and attention and affection to become absorbed and involved.

Verbalize

It is wise for engaged couples to begin talking about the sexual part of marriage two or three months before the wedding. This has many advantages. It develops a habit of talking about the physical relationship. Those couples who have a difficult time appropriately talking about sex before they are married may well develop a pattern of avoiding it, and this is extremely difficult to correct later. Most couples experience sexual attraction during their engagement, and when they deny the existence of these feelings or exclude them from their conversation, they are con cealing important parts of themselves from each other. Another advantage of talking about this part of a relationship before marriage is that getting it into the open will help you each control yourself so you will not go beyond the levels of intimacy that are appropriate for an engaged couple.

A third reason to begin talking about sex is that a couple can begin to deal with their fears and anxieties. Usually both the man and woman have these fears and anxieties. The woman is frequently apprehensive about whether the man will be too forceful, whether there will be discomfort for her in the sex act, whether he will be considerate enough to stop and not go further if she needs this, whether their bodies will be compatible with regard to size, etc. The man frequently has apprehensions about whether he will be embarrassed, whether they will be compatible, whether he will be adequate, etc. The male ego is usually very highly involved in how adequate he will be, and many men do not realize how emotionally involved they are with these concerns. Talking together can help you tremendously as a couple as you work through these feelings.

After you are married, you will spend years adjusting to and learning about the sexual part of your relationship. You will learn how to help each other respond. You will learn what you enjoy and do not enjoy, and how to respond to each other differently at different times. For example, the wife may respond differently in some parts of the menstrual cycle than in other parts, and she may want her husband to behave differently. Also, he may respond differently when unusual things happen in his employment. You will also learn how to use the sexual part of your relationship for different purposes. Sometimes it can be a romantic experience, and at other times a spiritual experience where you are trying to create a new body, to create a new tabernacle for a spirit. At other times the sexual embrace can be used to express feelings of love, to make up, to show support, for relaxation, for pleasure. You have many things to learn about each other, and you will be able to develop and grow and learn for many years in the sexual part of your relationship.

How can you expect to learn all these things as well as learn how to relate to each other if you don't talk about this important part of your lives?

You can't.

So . . . you must talk, talk, talk, talk!

Create Security

Researchers have found that feelings of security about one's spouse will influence one's sexual interaction. This is especially true for the wife. When a wife feels that she can trust her husband to be faithful, when she can "count on" the stability of their love, she feels free to invest herself more in the sexual experience. The result is that she enjoys the intimate moments more and is better able to attain sexual fulfillment.

Enjoy Physical Contact

Researchers have also found that the enjoyment of sensory contact is an important part of physical interaction in marriage. Some husbands and wives feel good about their bodies and they enjoy a wide variety of physical contact. They each feel pleasure when close to the other, and they love to snuggle, hold hands, and touch each other. They are also sensitive to the pleasant *feelings* they have when they are thirsty and have a long cold drink of water — a sensory pleasure. They notice that it *feels* good to take a rest after strong physical exertion — a sensory pleasure. At other times, such as when they are waking up or are just going to sleep, they pause to soak up the pleasure of the moment. On a beautiful spring day they stop as they walk by a beautiful scene, just to let it soak in. This habit of enjoying physical sensations of pleasure has many advantages. One advantage is that it seems to help a person be a responsive sex partner in marriage.

Some people are just the opposite. They do not like their physical bodies and do not think they should take pleasure in them. They may experience great joy from other things such as service, reading, music, or doing something well, but they avoid the feelings of pleasure that accompany the body. Perhaps they have been taught that bodily pleasures have a touch of evil to them. This pattern of avoiding or denying physical pleasures usually interferes with the sexual part of one's life. It may keep a person from being an effective sex partner with his spouse, at best depriving the couple of gratifications that are natural and proper, at worst raising physical roadblocks that make the sex act unsatisfying, uncomfortable, or even impossible. Either way the couple will miss out on a source of mutual tenderness and fulfillment that can be very beautiful and can promote feelings of love and attraction.

Get Help When You Need It

The sexual part of marriage is so intricate and complex that there are many things that can keep it from functioning properly. Physical abnormalities such as a growth or deformity in the reproductive organs can disrupt these processes. Emotional problems of any type can interfere with these delicate parts of life. In addition, there are a number of other psychological problems either the husband or the wife, or both, may have that can disrupt normal sexual interaction. They are unwise stewards when, having problems such as these in the sexual part of their lives, they decide to ignore them by not seeking help.

There are a number of different places you can turn to for help if you experience these problems. If your problem seems to be physical in nature, you would do well to get help from a medical doctor. An obstetrician or gynecologist, and many times a doctor in general or family practice, can be most helpful. If your problem deals with spiritual matters, you ought to seek help from your bishop or stake president. You may have feelings of guilt or un-worthiness or inadequacy, and when these are corrected your life will return to normal. If your problems deal with your interaction with your spouse, or with your emotions, or if you are not sure what your problems are, there is a new specialty in the counseling profession that can be very helpful. Many counselors have been trained in the techniques of sex therapy that have been emerging in the last two decades, and they can help you determine what your problems are and how you can best solve them.

It is important for Latter-day Saint couples to know that coun-selors who deal with sex problems differ a great deal in their sensi-tivity to LDS beliefs. Some clinics offering sex therapy are very worldly organizations that advocate grossly immoral and unwise sexual practices. Some of them do not appreciate the LDS phi-losophy that the sexual part of life is a very private and personal area that should be revered; and they do not share the Latter-day Saint belief that sexual interaction should be exclusively confined to marriage. Fortunately, however, there are many counselors and clinics who do recognize and respect LDS beliefs, and they offer professional assistance that is consistent with your views. In most areas of the United States there are LDS counselors who are well trained who personally share your beliefs and are also profes-sionally competent. Some of these counselors are bishops or stake presidents or hold other leadership positions in the Church.

This means that you need to be extremely careful in seeking professional assistance in this area. Many medical doctors have received no training to deal with sexual problems, and they are no more proficient in this respect than your next-door neighbor. In many states, counselors do not have to receive any training at all and they do not have to be licensed. You therefore need to be very cautious in obtaining professional assistance in this area.

Summary

This chapter has allowed you to consider, within an eternal perspective, the appropriate ways to sexually respond to your spouse. While this discussion has been open and forthright, it is hoped that each of you has gained an appreciation for your body, your emotions, and your personal responsibility in dealing with this area of your marriage.

While Satan has polluted our world so that it is difficult to know what is appropriate and what is not, your protection will come, finally, from an earnest effort to allow the Holy Ghost to become operative in this part of your marriage. When you approach the sexual union with reverence and respect, and with a selfless desire to be concerned about your partner, then not only will your physical relationship grow and flourish but your entire relationship will experience satisfaction and fulfillment. It is hoped that as you approach your wedding day, this information will stand you in good stead and allow your marriage to begin in a proper, positive, and trusting environment.

7

Infatuation is when you think that he's as sexy as Robert Redford, as smart as Henry Kissinger, as noble as Ralph Nader, as funny as Woody Allen and as athletic as Jimmy Connors. Love is when you realize that he's as sexy as Woody Allen, as smart as Jimmy Connors, as funny as Ralph Nader, as athletic as Henry Kissinger and nothing like Robert Redford in any category — but you'll take him anyway. (Vorst.)

Creating and Nurturing Love Feelings

Ahh . . . LOVE! The most peaceful, exciting, thrilling — and yet troublesome — part of life. There are no other feelings like it, and everyone wants to be "in love!"

While you are engaged, what should you do about your love feelings . . . other than enjoy them? There are two things that are wise to do. First, it is useful to learn what your particular style of loving is. There are many different styles of loving, and a little insight into this irrational and emotional part of life can help it be pleasant rather than frustrating. The second thing you can do is learn how to foster and enhance your love feelings. First, what is your style of love like?

Styles of Love

Research about love suggests that there are six basic dimensions or "colors" to love. (There are undoubtedly many more, but this is a manageable and useful list.) In simple terms they are:

1. The romantic part. This is the part that gives us tingles and that warm feeling in the heart. It sweeps us off our feet and is the part emphasized in movies and novels.

2. The friendship part. This is the part that is more calm and relaxed, but it makes us want to do things with the other person. Sometimes our loved one is also our "best friend."

3. The possessive part. This part makes us want to cling to the other person and makes us jealous when others get too close to him or her.

4. The sensible part. This is the part wherein we observe that we are good for each other, well matched, and that the love will not be an "easy come, easy go" thing.

5. The altruistic part. This is the part that makes us want to do things for the other person. It prompts us to be willing to "give-in" and to be kind, considerate, and patient.

6. The game-playing part. This is the part wherein we like surprises and the unpredictable. It is the dimension in which we like to keep an unknown element.

Two scholars have developed a questionnaire that can help you know how you combine these six dimensions into your unique style of loving. Before talking about these styles further, it is a good idea for you to answer the questions. (It is fun and will give you an interesting picture.)

To get the most benefit from this activity, don't try to paint a rosy picture. Tell it like it is! Mark the questions separately, without the other person knowing how you marked them until you're both through.

T   F   1. I believe that "love at first sight" is possible.

T   F   2. I did not realize that I was in love until I actually had been for some time.

T   F   3. When things aren't going right for us, my stomach gets upset.

T   F   4. From a practical point of view, I must consider what a person is going to become in life before I commit myself to loving him/her.

T F 5. You cannot have love unless you have first had a caring for awhile.

T F 6. It's always a good idea to keep the one you love a little uncertain about how committed you are to him/her.

T F 7. I still have good friendships with almost everyone with whom I have ever been involved in a love relationship.

T F 8. It makes good sense to plan your life carefully before you choose to love a person.

T F 9. When my romances break up I get so depressed that I have even thought of suicide.

T F 10. Sometimes I get so excited about being in love that I can't sleep.

T F 11. I try to use my own strength to help my loved one through difficult times, even when he/she is behaving foolishly.

T F 12. I would rather suffer myself than let my loved one suffer.

T F 13. Part of the fun of being in love is testing one's skills at keeping it going and getting what one wants from it at the same time.

T F 14. As far as my loved one goes, what he/she doesn't know about me won't hurt her/him.

T F 15. It is best to love someone who has a similar background.

T F 16. We kissed each other soon after we met because we both wanted to.

T F 17. When my loved one doesn't pay attention to me I feel sick all over.

T F 18. I cannot be happy unless I place my loved one's happiness before my own.

T F 19. The first thing that usually attracts my attention to a person is his/her pleasing physical appearance.

T	F	20.	The best kind of love grows out of a long friendship.
T	F	21.	When I am in love I have trouble concentrating on anything else.
T	F	22.	At the first touch of his/her hand I knew that love was a real possibility.
T	F	23.	When I break up with someone I go out of my way to see that he/she is okay.
T	F	24.	I cannot relax if I suspect that he/she is with someone else.
T	F	25.	At least once I have had to plan carefully to keep two people I loved from finding out about each other.
T	F	26.	I can get over romances pretty easily and quickly.
T	F	27.	A main consideration in choosing a partner is whether or not he/she will be a good parent.
T	F	28.	The best part of love is living together, building a home together, and rearing children together.
T	F	29.	I am usually willing to sacrifice my own wishes to let the one I love achieve his/hers.
T	F	30.	Kissing and cuddling shouldn't be rushed. They will happen naturally when one's relationship has grown enough.
T	F	31.	I enjoy flirting with attractive people.
T	F	32.	The one I love would get upset if he/she knew some of the things I've done with other people.
T	F	33.	Before I ever fell in love I had a pretty clear understanding of what true love would be like.
T	F	34.	If the one I love had a baby by someone else I would want to raise it, love it, and care for it as if it were my own.
T	F	35.	It is hard to say exactly when we fell in love.
T	F	36.	I couldn't truly love anyone I would not be willing to marry.
T	F	37.	Even though I don't want to be jealous, I can't help it when the one I love pays attention to someone else.

T	F	38.	I would rather break up with the one I love than to stand in his/her way.
T	F	39.	I like the idea of having the same kinds of clothes, hats, plants, bicycles, cars, etc.
T	F	40.	I wouldn't date anyone that I wouldn't want to fall in love with.
T	F	41.	At least once when I thought a romance was all over, I saw him/her again and the old feeling came surging back.
T	F	42.	Whatever I own belongs to the one I love to use as he/she chooses.
T	F	43.	When I am with the one I love I feel "swept off my feet."
T	F	44.	It would be fun to see whether I can get someone to go out with me even if I didn't want to get involved with that person.
T	F	45.	A main consideration in choosing a partner is how he/she will reflect on one's career.
T	F	46.	The best love relationships are the ones that last the longest.

The way to score this questionnaire is to circle on the accompanying Style of Loving chart each number for which you have indicated a "T" on the questionnaire. Then, for each column on the chart, write the total number of items circled. The higher the total for any column, the more important that dimension is for you; and the lower the total, the less important that dimension is for you. The scorers therefore will give you a "profile" of your particular style of loving.

There are several interesting things you can learn from this exercise. You can see if your "style" of loving is similar to what you thought it was before you completed the exercise. And if the questionnaire is different from what you thought, you can talk about why. Maybe the questionnaire only sampled a few things and it doesn't give the complete picture for you.

You can also see how similar the two profiles are. Is her profile similar to or different from his? If they are similar, this suggests that you like the same style of love. If they are different, this suggests that you may have different needs. One may need more romance or possessiveness than the other, or may be different in other ways. It is very possible for two people to have different styles. And when you are aware of these differences, you can probably meet each other's needs better.

Style of Loving

Romantic	Friendship	Possessive	Sensible	Altruistic	Game Playing
1	2	6	4	11	3
7	5	13	8	12	9
16	7	14	15	18	10
19	20	25	27	23	17
22	28	26	30	29	21
33	30	31	36	34	24
39	35	32	40	38	37
43	46	44	45	42	41

Totals

_____ _____ _____ _____ _____ _____

The greatest benefit of this exercise is that you can use it as a springboard to a long and thorough talk about your love and your style of loving. You can discuss the many different aspects of your love that are not tapped by the questionnaire and learn more and more about each other. As you do you'll probably come closer together, even though you may learn some new things about each other. And the whole process of learning about each other can help your love to grow even stronger.

Enhancing Love Feelings

There is a "general principle" that can help you enhance your love feelings. It is:

The profit principle: The more profitable your interaction, the stronger your love.

The key word in this principle is *profit*. What does it mean? It is the balance of rewards and costs. It is similar to the profit in a business or company — income (rewards) minus expenses (costs).

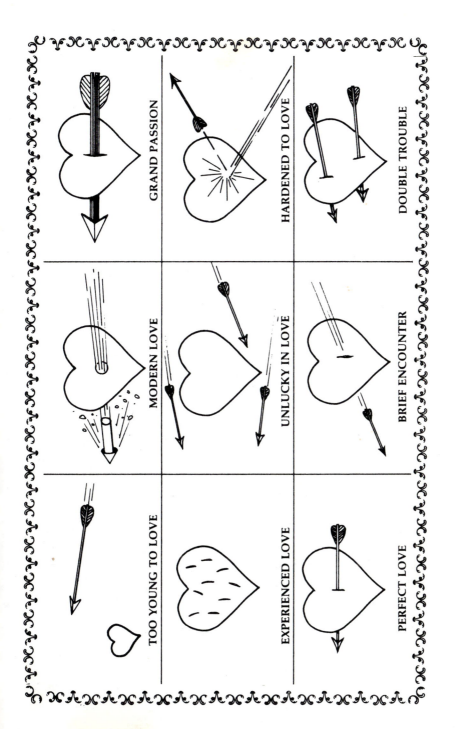

GRAND PASSION

HARDENED TO LOVE

DOUBLE TROUBLE

MODERN LOVE

UNLUCKY IN LOVE

BRIEF ENCOUNTER

TOO YOUNG TO LOVE

EXPERIENCED LOVE

PERFECT LOVE

But the rewards and costs in relationships are not limited to money. In fact, the economic rewards and costs in marriage are usually a minor part of the total. In marriage, contentment, security, acceptance, pride, being needed, assistance, mutual fulfillment, and being cared for are some of the important rewards. Hurt pride, deflated self-esteem, rejection, loneliness, and frustration are some of the important costs.

So . . . how can you use this principle? There are three ways to use it, and they are:

1. Increase rewarding things in your relationship.
2. Decrease costly things in your relationship.
3. Continue to "interact" a lot.

Let's talk about each of these three in more detail.

Increase Rewards

First of all, surroundings are important. You usually learn to like people who are associated with good times, and you often dislike people who are associated with bad times. If you interact with a person only in unpleasant surroundings, that person becomes associated with unpleasantness, and you may tend to develop negative feelings about him.

This is one of the reasons why it is so easy for love feelings to develop when dating. You dress up, act polite, go to fascinating places, meet new people, and are usually surrounded by a romantic atmosphere. This is also a reason why some married couples fall out of love as the years pass. They gradually develop patterns in which they interact only with their problems. "Johnny broke the window." "Sue needs braces." "Whom will we get for a babysitter tonight?" "The bills are due." "Your mother isn't coming to stay again, is she?" "Jerry dented the fender; and he was called in by the principal, is running with the wrong group, and doesn't go to sacrament meeting?" Do these words sound familiar? If these things become associated with your interaction, your marriage will lose its luster rapidly.

What does this mean for dating and marriage?

It means that if you want romance in your love relationship, you need to do romantic things as often as possible and avoid or minimize nonromantic things. You will need romantic dinners;

trips to the theatre, evenings at home with soft music; appreciation and thanks; vacations together; dressing up to go out; little surprises; and lots of those soft, sweet sentiments that everyone likes to hear. It means that when problems come, you need to solve them and put them behind you rather than let them drag on unsolved. It means that you need to forgive and forget often and quickly.

Some couples aren't too concerned about continuing romance but do want to have strong feelings of companionate love. What does this idea mean for you? It means lots of time for talks about things that are pleasant, positive, and dear to you both—taking the time to share precious feelings; doing the little things that your spouse enjoys, such as buying special perfume; pausing for a few minutes on the way home from work so that you won't take the troubles of the office home with you; remembering to say good-bye in a way your spouse will remember; and including please and thank you as you interact. You ought not to associate your spouse with wet towels thoughtlessly dropped on the floor; complaints about the things you haven't been able to get done yet; crying and nagging; guilt feelings; barked-out orders; resentments; jealousies; and the little, nagging feeling as you or your partner comes home . . . What will it be this time?

The key: We love the things which are associated with good times. We learn to dislike those associated with bad times.

Create Sense of Importance

One central theme in much social science literature is that people desire and strive for a feeling that they belong. People need to be important to at least a small group of other people. Erich Fromm's writings about freedom and love emphasize the significance of this sense of belonging. This idea is relevant as it pertains to marriage because a person finds it extremely rewarding (highly profitable) to feel important to others—not for what these others can do for him, but for what he is as a person. A sense of importance is an emotional value. It is what a person feels and how he makes others feel.

There are many ways to tell how important you are to each other, and there are some ways to increase or decrease this sense of importance. One thing that provides clues is the amount of attention you pay to your companion. When people are of little importance to you, you will likely pay little attention to such things as their opinions, concerns, wishes, or feelings. But when they are more important, they receive more of your attention.

One trap you may fall into at times is telling yourself that someone is important but that you aren't able to show this as much as you desire to. You have to do such and such at the office, or there are such and such demands around the house. In actual fact, what you frequently tell yourself is that the other person is more important to you than he really may be. The way you act is usually a more accurate indicator of how important to you someone really is than the self-deceiving things you may tell yourself about how important he is.

A sense of others' importance is subtle. It may seem a small part of life, but it makes a big difference and is easily shown. The following incident told by Emma Ray Riggs McKay illustrates its visibility and importance.

> "I accompanied my husband to a dedication of a meetinghouse in Los Angeles. We stopped on Wilshire Boulevard to get our car washed. I sat on a bench and the President was standing over by the car. Suddenly at my elbow I heard a tiny voice say, 'I guess that man over there loves you.' Surprised, I turned and saw a beautiful boy about seven years of age with dark curly hair and large brown eyes. 'What did you say?'
>
> " 'I said, I guess that man over there loves you.'
>
> " 'Why, yes, he loves me; he is my husband. Why do you ask?'
>
> " 'Oh, 'cuz, the way he smiled at you. Do you know, I'd give anything in the world if my Pop would smile at my Mom that way.'
>
> " 'Oh, I'm sorry he doesn't,' I said.
>
> " 'I guess you're not going to get a divorce, then.'
>
> " 'Oh, no, we're not going to get a divorce. We've been married nearly fifty years, and we are very happy. Why do you think that?'
>
> " 'Oh, 'cuz everybody gets a divorce around here. My Pop is going to get a divorce from my Mom. I love my Pop and Mom, and I' — his voice broke and tears welled in his eyes, but he was too much of a little man to let them fall.
>
> "Then he came very close and whispered confidentially in my ear, 'You'd better hurry out of Los Angeles, or you'll get a divorce too.' And he picked up his papers and shuffled down the sidewalk."
> ("The Art of Rearing Children Peacefully" [BYU Press, 1966], p. 10;

as quoted in Paul H. Dunn, Maurine Ward, *Look at Your World* [Bookcraft, 1978].)

Decrease Costs

Another way you can increase your total profit is to decrease the costs in your interaction. Costly things are unpleasant, negative, or undesirable. No one can eliminate all of the costs in their lives, but they can reduce many of them. They can look at how they behave and determine where there are costs that they can reduce. The following list describes some things that can be done.

Ways to Reduce Costs and Increase Rewards in Interaction
— Don't belittle one another in public.
— Do what the other wants to do often.
— Create a pleasant atmosphere in the home.
— Avoid gossiping about each other.
— Maintain personal cleanliness.
— Support, motivate, and increase one another's self-esteem.
— Greet each other pleasantly at the end of the day.
— Let the other person know your schedule.
— Keep your own messes cleaned up.
— Be punctual.
— Do not jump to conclusions.
— Be tolerant of another's faults.
— Acknowledge positive feelings.
— Be aware of menstrual cycle.
— Keep up physical appearance.
— Be interested in one another's projects.
— Be tolerant of each other's viewpoint.
— Show an interest in each other's daily activities.
— Remember important dates.
— Compliment one another.
— Eliminate complaints to one another.
— Be to dinner on time.
— Try not to nag.
— Keep one another's confidences.
— Take time to listen; stop other activities when listening.
— Respect the other's time schedule.
— Keep up your end of role expectations.

— Be aware of one another's commitments.
— Be appreciative.
— Be aware of one another's priorities.
— Don't interrupt each other.
— Don't criticize one another's friends.
— Budget money wisely.
— Always be courteous.
— Fulfill individual responsibilities.
— Allow husband and wife time to relax after coming home from work.
— Support partner in discipline of children.

Here is an exercise that can help you identify some costly behaviors that you may have in your relationship. If you find that you are doing any of these things too frequently, you can probably increase your love feelings by decreasing these costs.

Identifying Areas of Costly Interaction

Write *seldom or never, occasionally,* or *frequently* in each of the blanks.

1. Nagging.   _____
2. "Uncommunicativeness," keeping our feel-
    ings inside.   _____
3. Conversational discourtesies; putting down
    and ridiculing each other.   _____
4. Being selfish.   _____
5. Attacking our partner instead of recognizing,
    labeling, expressing, and owning our own
    feelings when we are angry.   _____
6. Disclosing feelings at inappropriate times,
    such as just before dinner, when there are
    distractions, lack of privacy, etc.   _____
7. Expressing negative feelings when we are
    not in control of ourselves.   _____
8. Expressing negative feelings when our part-
    ner is not in control of him/herself.   _____
9. Not using tact, love, consideration; dumping
    too much at once when expressing negative
    emotions.   _____

10. Being inconsistent in our verbal and nonverbal communications. Our words say one thing and our actions say something different. _____
11. Failing to listen attentively and to use eye contact, and thinking about what we are going to say next instead of concentrating on what the other is saying. _____
12. Failing to recognize nonverbal messages, such as gestures and facial expressions. _____
13. Failing to "check out" what we hear to be sure that we've heard correctly. _____
14. Rejecting our partner's feelings — "You couldn't possibly feel like that." _____
15. Being quick to anger. _____
16. Refusing to accept responsibility. _____
17. Being stubborn. _____
18. Being domineering. _____
19. Being prone to prolonged moods of sadness, anger, or boredom. _____
20. Having an "unrighteous pride."
21. Trying to be one up on the other. _____
22. Being easily hurt when constructive criticism is given to you. _____
23. Failing to accept responsibility for faults and blaming others. _____
24. Being unwilling to work on improving the relationship. _____
25. Having feelings of low self-esteem and personal worth. _____
26. Being impatient. _____
27. Not honoring priesthood and Church responsibilities. _____
28. Having less than an 80 percent to 20 percent ratio of positive, uplifting comments to such negative communication as giving insults, using rude words, and sarcasm. _____
29. Ignoring our partner's comments. _____

30. Being defensive instead of trying to understand our partner. _____
31. Spending too much time with and disclosing confidences to friends instead of one's spouse. _____
32. Using work as an escape to avoid coming home. _____
33. Having a lasting feeling of dissatisfaction. _____
34. Being indifferent to each other's problems. _____
35. Displaying occasions of coldness.
36. Avoiding or refusing sexual relations. _____
37. Taking too little interest in things of the other. _____
38. Being unkind and discourteous. _____
39. Lacking in tenderness. _____
40. Having feelings of insecurity and mutual distrust. _____
41. Lacking intimate communication. _____
42. Communicating on a mechanical, routine, surface level. _____
43. Feeling alone and not understood. _____
44. Displaying bad humor. _____
45. Quarreling in private and in public. _____
46. Escaping from each other through TV, prescription drugs, compulsive socializing, or too much work in the Church. _____
47. Being inactive in Church. _____
48. Lacking appreciation. _____
50. Not planning things together. _____
51. Avoiding situations that greatly need attention. _____
52. Failing to work through problems successfully. _____
53. Lacking unity in the relationship. _____
54. Not living up to the others expectations as to how one should behave. _____
55. Not leading the family with a spirit of charity as is specified in D&C 121:37-44. _____

56. Not considering the other's opinion in important decisions. _____
57. Not stating views in a tentative manner so as to communicate to the other that his opinions are important. _____
58. Being unable to compromise. _____
59. Being unwilling to give in on an issue for the good of the relationship. _____
60. Attempting to resolve difficult issues without the help of the Lord. _____
61. Lacking trust in each other. _____
62. Being a poor money manager. _____
63. Lacking in common goals and interests. _____

Assuming that this exercise is valid and useful, you can then each learn new ways to use it. The following pages identify things you can do to increase the profit in your relation.

Interact

Interact is a simple word, but it has far-reaching consequences. You will have few rewards in a relationship if you don't interact. It is only when you spend time sharing yourself and your experiences and doing things together that you will get pleasure from a relationship.

Most couples interact a great deal when they are dating, engaged, and first married. Later, as they become more settled in marriage, as babies come and job demands increase, most spend less and less time interacting. As mortgage payments become due, and church and civic responsibilities increase, these other activities and problems take more and more of our time, effort, and energy. Couples don't decide to interact less, they just find themselves doing it. They see less and less of each other. And then they wonder why the luster and glow of their love feelings sometimes fade.

Researchers found that unsatisfied couples disclosed more unpleasant feelings to each other, whereas satisfied couples disclosed more positive feelings. Such studies lend support to the profit principle. For most couples, though, it does not take formal research to make this notion convincing. Few couples will stay in any kind of relationship in which the outcomes are continually negative. Many people have resigned from jobs in which a boss has been overbearing and insensitive. Missionaries have a difficult time appreciating companions who are continually criticizing them and will request transfers. Students have been known to drop classes in which the teachers have insulted them. Children have run away from home situations wherein they receive more criticism than praise. And, yes, marriage partners have packed their bags and left their spouses when the criticism and put-downs were no longer tolerable.

Less interaction . . . less profit . . . less love!

There are several things you can do to correct this trend. First, if the love in your marriage is as important as you say it is, you can resolve now that you will plan your life so that you will spend profitable time interacting, enjoying, and sharing. You can decide right now that one evening a week will be your night out. You don't have to spend a lot of money on big social activities on these nights; they can be inexpensive activities or walks or talks. The important thing is that you spend the time with each other and demonstrate by your actions that you care. This advice has been given by our Church leaders for many years. Typical of the counsel given are the following comments:

> Those who allow the marriage ceremony to terminate the days of "courtship" are making a well-nigh fatal mistake. If the new bride were to discover that her husband was just an actor before their marriage and now his quest is ended he stands revealed as a cheap counterfeit of his former self either in appearance or conduct, that would indeed be a shocking experience. Evidences and tokens of your love and a daily proof of your unselfishness toward her and your family will make love's flame burn more brightly with the years. Do you girls suppose that the same attention to personal details is less important after marriage? Surely the same qualities and traits in you that first attracted him are just as important in married life in keeping alive the flame of his affection and romantic desire. (Harold B. Lee, *Decisions for Successful Living* [Salt Lake City: Deseret Book Company, 1973], pp. 173-174.)

President Spencer W. Kimball gave similar advice when he said:

> Love is like a flower, and, like the body, it needs constant feeding. The mortal body would soon be emaciated and die if there were not frequent feedings. The tender flower would wither and die without food and water. And so love, also, cannot be expected to last forever unless it is continually fed with portions of love, the manifestation of esteem and admiration, the expressions of gratitude, and the consideration of unselfishness. (*Marriage and Divorce*, pp. 22-23.)

Statements like these have been made by Church leaders since the early days of the Church. To continue courtship is the single most repeated counsel as to what it takes to have a successful marriage. Leaders have repeatedly told couples to take the time to interact with their spouses.

A Paradoxical Principle About Giving

A paradox is a statement that seems self-contradictory or absurd but is really consistent and true. Life has many paradoxes. For example, the more we seek happiness the less we may find it, because happiness is a by-product of doing right. And, he that seeketh his life shall lose it, but he that loseth his life shall find it.

Love, too, has its paradoxes. As the profit principle suggests, we love when we are rewarded. We love when we get what we want, when we have pleasure rather than pain. The paradox is that the opposite is also true—for reasons we may not understand. *Sacrificing, giving, and serving also build love feelings.*

The patient care that parents give their children is demanding. It is a sacrifice of many things, their time, effort, energy, independence, and freedom. And in almost everything that can be measured, it is mostly a one-way giving all through the years of child rearing. In fact, it is an immensely costly process to rear children—costly in economic terms and in emotional energy, commitment, devotion, patience, endurance, understanding, and time. It is true that there are great rewards in rearing children—rewards of joy and fulfillment. But when the daily interaction is examined, the costs are also extremely high. What, then, are the fruits of these sacrifices? Hate? Dislike? Indifference? Usually it isn't! Strong love feelings grow, and they grow partly because of what the parents give. Those parents who give little of themselves in this process create little love. But those who lose themselves in giving and serving, without ever expecting reimbursement, build the strongest love feelings.

This does not invalidate the profit principle. It also applies. There *are* parts of us that are hedonistic; and profit (rewards less costs) in our relationships builds love. Paradoxically, though, a contradictory principle is *also* true. The principle is:

> *The giving principle: The more we give to another person, especially of ourselves, the more we have love feelings for that person. (And the less we give, the less the feeling of love.)*

Giving can take many forms. It can be the giving of energy and service to the one we love (or want to love). It can be giving in frequently and doing things the other person's way most of the time rather than our way. It can be giving him attention and encouragement and care when he is low or troubled or discouraged. It can be giving up something that we want so that he can have something he wants. It can be worrying about his welfare, making sure his needs are met.

The cynic may worry that giving a great deal may lead to one-way exploitation, and in some situations this can become a problem, especially in political and business situations. In dating, marriage, and family life, it can be a problem when we are giving materialistic things; but when we are giving of ourselves, it is almost never a problem. *It is a solution to problems.*

What usually happens in marriage and family life is that Deutsch's Law takes over: when one person becomes a truly "giving" person. *The desire to give spreads to others.* Very few couples have those rare problems that come from too much giving; they have the more numerous and common problems that come from too little. They worry about getting rather than giving, and as a result they behave in getting rather than giving ways—and then wonder why their love feelings become stale or wither and die. The solutions? Here are a few ideas:

1. Worry about what your spouse gets more than about what you get.
2. Give in much more than seems to be your share.
3. When your spouse wants something badly, try to find a way to get it.
4. Spouses are to be spoiled. Try it; it makes them nicer.
5. Me less; him/her more.
6. Listen carefully when your spouse says, "I wish you would . . . ." And then try hard to do it because he or she wants it.
7. Balance the luxuries in your lives so that she/he gets the lion's share.
8. Do it her/his way.

The giving principle can help you better understand and apply the ideas on charity in chapter two. The Savior discussed this process of giving rather than getting when He preached the Sermon on the Mount. He taught that we ought to return good for evil, turn the other cheek, give up our cloaks, go the second mile, and forgive seventy times seven. These teachings seem to be based on unnatural ways of behaving. Our natural impulses are either to get our own way more than the other person gets his (as many try to do in business) or to use rules of justice and fair play and evenly distribute good and bad things. Both ways of behaving are inferior to the Lord's higher method of returning good for evil; and His method is the best if we want loving relationships. There is no place these teachings have more relevance than in preparing for a marriage relationship. Consider the following situations, for example:

If my spouse is tired, irritable, and cross,	should I	retaliate with angry words? or bite my tongue for a while and help out, then at a later time acknowledge that it was a little hard to do it?
If my spouse is critical of something I've done,	should I	criticize something he/she has done to justify myself? or admit my mistake and thank my spouse for his/her interest in helping me improve?

If my spouse is angry at something,	should I	get angry too? or count to ten, take a few deep breaths, or do something else to keep control; then, after the situation is over, talk peacefully about what happened?
If my spouse wants a new sofa but I don't,	should I	fight for my opinion? or be more willing to give in and do it his/her way?
If my spouse wants the car cleaner and straighter,	should I	ignore the wish or bring up something I want too? or go along with his/her wish?
If my spouse criticized me in front of someone and I was embarrased,	should I	lash out or criticize or make fun? or nicely try to make the best of the situation and later talk about my feelings and ask my spouse to criticize me in private?
If my spouse hasn't done several things I asked,	should I	get mad, yell, or coerce? or try to talk about my feelings about it without hurting him/her?
If my spouse is having a difficult time living one of the commandments,	should I	keep after him/her to do better or flaunt my righteousness in that area? or think about, focus on, talk about expressing appreciation for the areas in which he/she isn't having a hard time, ignoring the problem area unless he/she wants me to say something or help?

| If my spouse isn't very kind to me, | should I | get even or be unkind back?
or
be more kind to my spouse than I have been? |
| If my spouse doesn't understand some of the things that are really important to me, | should I | ignore the things that are important to her/him?
or
try to be as understanding as I can, even try to increase my understanding? |

Most couples have learned the cultural traditions that are dominant in the twentieth century. And, unfortunately, many of these traditions are inconsistent with the eternal teachings of the Savior. They have learned to emphasize materialistic and economic values, such as getting as much as they can. And they've added some rationalizations that make this attitude seem compatible with Christ's teachings. For example, they tell themselves that they should emphasize economic values so that they can do "good" with the money they receive. They also have learned well the processes of justice and fairness, at a level of perfection just slightly above the Law of Moses. The parts of the Savior's teachings that focus on returning good for evil, absorbing criticisms and injustices and returning positive responses to them, and treating others as we would like to be treated, are almost foreign ideas in our culture. In our "natural" condition, the natural thing to do is to exploit or abuse or at most be fair and just. *As you are able to learn and then live the higher law of giving good no matter what, you will elevate yourself, your marriage, your family, your ward, your community, your nation, and your world.* And you will create love feelings for those with whom you interact.

Summary

This chapter was concerned with what you can do to create love feelings. Two ideas were presented: The first part of the chapter dealt with the *profit principle*, which states that the greater the profit (rewards less costs) in your interaction with someone, the greater your love feelings. Ways to increase the profit in your interaction were then presented. The last part of the chapter introduced a paradoxical principle about giving to others. It was called the *giving principle,* and it stated that the more you give to someone else (service, sacrifice) the more you will have love feelings for him.

As authors, we wish you the very best as you grow in your capacity to love. Consider now an even different type of love.

The Lord God hath given a
commandment that all men should
have charity, which charity is
love. And except they should
have charity they were nothing.
(2 Nephi 26:30.)

8

Fashioning Love With Love

As you continue your journey toward marriage, it becomes increasingly important for you to step briefly away from your engagement to consider relationships in general. The nature of this exploration becomes crystal clear in the admonition of the Lord recorded by Matthew (22:36-39) wherein the two great commandments are presented. To love and totally respect the Lord is the greatest commandment, with the second being to love our neighbor as ourselves.

This love of mankind is often referred to in the scriptures as *charity* or the pure love of Christ (Moroni 7:47). Some of its components include benevolence, compassion, generosity, love of God, and mercy.

Unfortunately, we live in a world today where the prediction is fulfilled that "the love of men shall wax cold, and iniquity shall abound" (D&C 45:27). We not only see examples of this in the warring of nations, but we also see it clearly in our own neighborhoods, as it seems that more and more of us have less and less patience for the mistakes and weaknesses of others. This tendency seems to have evolved as we have collectively turned inward, concerning ourselves only with our personal pleasures and needs.

Even so, as Latter-day Saints we know charity to be the foundation upon which all successful relationships (and therefore successful marriages) are built. Should you fail to acquire this trait and subsequently negotiate your marriage without it, it will be like trying to cross the ocean in a sailboat without a rudder. It is going to be almost impossible for you to weather the inevitable marital storms.

The Importance of Charity

The underlying importance of charity was emphasized by Paul as he said:

> And though I have the gift of prophecy, and understand all mysteries, and all knowledge; and though I have all faith, so that I could remove mountains, and have not charity, I am nothing. (1 Corinthians 13:2.)

Nephi expressed similar sentiments when he proclaimed,

> The Lord God hath given a commandment that all men should have charity, which charity is love. And except they should have charity they were nothing. (2 Nephi 26:30.)

A married couple who has the ability to do all else well, including such important things as church activity, financial solvency, communication skills, etc., but *has not charity* is "as sounding brass, or a tinkling cymbal" (1 Corinthians 13:1). In other words, such a marriage is empty, hollow, and incomplete. Expressed positively, charity should become the foundation upon which you strive to build your marriage, for without it none of the other attributes you carry into marriage will be of worth to you.

What Does It Mean to Be Charitable in Marriage?

Being a charitable couple is more than holding hands and embracing often, although this is a beginning. In combining the wisdom and understanding of Paul and Moroni, you will find a more complete picture of what charity should mean in your approaching marriage. These great men use many phrases in 1 Corinthians 13 and Moroni 7 to define charity. From this perspective these characteristics of love can be divided into three main themes which can better help you understand how you can be more charitable toward your eternal companion. The themes are (1) that we should be concerned about others rather than be selfish, (2) that we should be patient and enduring with ourselves and others, and (3) that we should be righteous in our hearts as well as in the way we behave.

Being Concerned About Others

Concern for others involves five separate behaviors: (1) seeketh not her own, (2) vaunteth not itself, (3) is not puffed up, (4) envieth not, and (5) is kind.

Simply stated, a couple who practice these positive behaviors care about each other, and their actions toward each other demonstrate this care. The opposite of these actions would be such behaviors as selfishness, conceit, egotism, uninvolvement, and being concerned only about oneself.

Our modern prophets have said much about the importance of being concerned about others. President Kimball has declared:

> The marriage that is based upon selfishness is almost certain to fail. . . . But the one who marries to give happiness as well as receive it, to give service as well as to receive it, and looks after the interests of the two and then the family as it comes will have a good chance that the marriage will be a happy one. . . . Total unselfishness is sure to accomplish another factor in successful marriage. If each spouse is forever seeking the interests, comforts, and happiness of the other, the love found in courtship and cemented in marriage will grow into mighty proportions. (*Marriage and Divorce*, pp. 22-23.)

This type of charitable love in marriage is a sure sign of maturity in both partners. To be able to place a relationship above one's own desires and needs is to have moved from childhood to manhood and womanhood. It is recognized by many as one of the basic steps toward being ready for marriage.

This linkage between maturity and charity was implied by Paul at the end of his sermon on the meaning of charity as he said:

> When I was a child, I spake as a child, I understood as a child, I thought as a child: but when I became a man, I put away childish things. (1 Corinthians 13:11.)

Could Paul have been saying that to be charitable a person needs to grow up? Is it immature to be selfish and self-centered? Perhaps we need only to look at the behavior of small children for the answers. Young children live in a self-centered world of their own "wants" while for the most part ignoring the needs of those around them. They want food when hungry, they want their diapers changed, they want the attention of parents, and they want another child's toys. They are not yet experienced or mature enough to be able to empathize — to vicariously feel what another feels. About the time most children start to develop this ability, they are baptized and are then held accountable for their actions.

Even so, some people develop empathy very slowly and marry with little ability to place themselves in the emotional shoes of their spouses. Typical marital *faux pas* of immature partners include these *true* incidents·

Incident 1: A husband, against his wife's wishes, purchased a new four-wheel drive pick-up, even though they were behind on their house payments. Rather than face the righteous wrath of his wife, he hid the pick-up at a friend's house.

Incident 2: A wife surprised her husband by inviting her family to a family reunion at their home. She had not asked her husband for permission because she knew he would not approve. The husband retaliated by doing obnoxious things that upset both his wife and her family.

Incident 3: A wife was so upset with her husband for never being at home or paying any attention to her that she took his new Buick, which she saw getting far more attention and care than she, and proceeded to drive it in a wreckless manner around and around the apartment building parking lot. When her husband came out and tried to stop her, she chased him around the parking lot in an attempt to run over him. As the police arrived she rammed into their cars and continued the chase until she came to rest, car and all, in the front room of one of the neighbors.

These couples could greatly benefit from learning to effectively and maturely deal with their feelings as well as to respond to the feelings of their spouses.

The first two aspects of being concerned about others, "seeketh not her own" and "vaunteth not itself," are closely related to unselfishness in meaning and practical application. The third, "is not puffed up," is more closely related to pride as we interact with others. In everyday actions it means such things as being more concerned about being "right" than about the feelings of our companions. Or when we have a difference of opinion with our spouses, we superficially listen only enough so that we can formulate our counterattacks. Or, when our spouses send a message that could be interpreted in a negative way, we take great offense and allow our "righteous" indignation to head toward the boiling level. Carried further, it could also mean refusing to quickly forgive our spouses for offending us — or even not to forgive them at all and to harbor ill feelings over an extended period of time.

The opposite of pride (being puffed up) is humility. To be humble in a marriage relationship is to be teachable and to admit that there may be a solution to the problem other than the one we have suggested. It is also to appreciate the subjective rightness of the other's point of view even though we "know" that it is incorrect when compared to our own view. A humble person is also teachable enough to be willing to compromise even though he feels his plan is superior; and at times he will even give in and let the other person have his own way simply because the relationship is more important than the problem. To do these things is difficult for most people and requires self-mastery and great maturity.

The fourth aspect of charity, it "envieth not," is defined as our ability to overcome the common temptation to compare ourselves to others and to compete with them. We live in a competitive world today wherein great emphasis is placed on winning, being number one. We see it not only in the athletic world but also in the business world, in schools, and elsewhere—sometimes including one's own marriage. There are situations in which this competition can be healthy and exciting, but marriage is usually *not* one of them.

Often when marriage partners compete with each other it is because one feels inferior to the other (or both do) because of a lack of self-esteem. When this happens one partner feels the need to criticize and otherwise try to put the other beneath his own perceived feelings of inferiority. Each mate uses the other as a means of feeling bigger—at the other's expense.

An example of this behavior is seen in the following dialogue of a young couple who sought counseling after only a few months of marriage. The wife felt that it was unfair that she be forced to do all the housework while the husband just sat around the house giving orders. In this episode the wife is trying to get her husband to help:

H: What do you want? Do you want to tune-up the car while I come in and do the dishes?

W: Well, not really, but all it is that I'm asking is that—(Husband interrupts.)

H: It doesn't take any skill or training to do the housework, now does it?

W: Not really. But I'm not asking you to do the dishes every night, I just want you to help every—(Husband interrupts.)

H: I never ask you to work on the car, do I?

W: No, but I just don't understand why we can't be more equal. I have to come home and hurry and fix your meal or you get angry with me, and you just sit there and watch TV. We work the same number of hours each day and I have worked just as hard as you do. Why can't you help me a little?

H: Well, what difference does it make? Who cares who makes the most money or who works the most hours each week? Housework is your responsibility because I gave you that assignment when we were married.

W: I still don't understand why we can't be equal.

H: It's because you're a woman, and I'm a man. You have your work, and I have mine.

Could this husband be guilty of using his wife to build his own ego by making his marriage a contest in which he always had to win? Why was it necessary for him to always be in control and to be above his wife and her needs? How would developing attributes of charity have helped this marriage?

The fifth aspect of being concerned about others is to show kindness to them. There are literally thousands of ways to do this. For husbands and wives it could mean refusing to be angry when the other is angry. Or it could mean making an effort to be more stimulating in conversation, to be more attractive, or to find something new and to share it with the other. It could be learning a new hobby, such as chess or skiing, just because the partner likes it, or giving compliments and encouragement, being affectionate, opening the door for the other, preparing a favorite dessert, or arranging a midweek luncheon date. The list is nearly endless.

An important way of showing kindness in marriage is to observe what some have called the rituals of respect. These include remembering and properly honoring our spouses on birthdays, Father's Day, Mother's Day, anniversaries, Christmas, and other special days. The effort that it takes to make these events memorable is well worth it in the strength of the bonds that are created.

As you know, many young couples go to great lengths in creating romantic rituals to prove their love and devotion to each other in the courtship stages. Proposals are seldom made in ordinary ways. One creative young man arranged for the student card section to flash the question "Will you marry me, Judy Campbell?" at half-time at a college football game. As if this wasn't dramatic enough, the startled girl looked around to see where her boyfriend was only to see everyone else looking up. They were looking at a hang glider soaring above the stadium. The glider gracefully descended upon the stadium and then landed right on the fifty-yard line. The pilot ran up the bleachers with all thirty-five thousand fans watching and presented the embarrassed girl with the engagement ring. The newspaper later confirmed her excited acceptance.

Another young couple had just finished eating at a Chinese restaurant when the fortune cookies were brought out. As the girl opened her cookie she was greatly surprised to find that her fortune read, "Marylyn, will you marry me? I love you, Doug." Next the Chinese cook came out of the kitchen carrying a dozen long-stemmed roses which he presented to her.

One of the authors, while courting his wife-to-be, found a heart-shaped cheese cake on the inside windowsill of his dorm room on Valentine's Day. What made this unusual was that the room was on the third floor. A ladder had been used to make the delivery early in the morning.

These experiences are all effective means of demonstrating love and commitment for building romances. In addition, these innovative rituals of love can provide opportunities for you, as the years pass, to further demonstrate your devotion to your spouse.

As important as it is to show these acts of kindness, it is just as important that there be an absence of unkind acts that may offset the good ones.

To tell a spouse "I love you" by arranging for a very special birthday party or by washing the dishes for her, and then to turn around the next day and nag at her for not taking out the garbage or for forgetting an errand, will not build the strong bonds of trust and affection that can come with consistent acts of kindness. For kindness and other acts of charity to have a lasting effect, they need to be performed in an environment in which unkind acts are rare and quickly repented of.

Paul states this point well in Romans 13:8-10:

> Owe no man any thing, but to love one another; for he that loveth another hath fulfilled the law. . . . Love worketh no ill to his neighbor: therefore love is the fulfilling of the law.

For love to be effective, it would appear that charitable acts must be done with an absence of uncharitable acts; for, as Paul says, true "love worketh no evil to his neighbor" (or his spouse).

Being Patient With Others

Patience is a dimension of charity. Moroni and Paul identified four parts of it: (1) it suffereth long; (2) it is not easily provoked; (3) it beareth all things; (4) it endureth all things.

In anticipating a Christlike marriage relationship, you can gain many insights by taking a positive view of these four concepts. As you do, think of patience not as being passive but as being active. Patience is not simply "putting up with" or "tolerating." It is *concentrated strength,* a strength to be counted on by your partner and others as a constant rather than an unknown. Mohammed once said that patience is the key to contentment. That is, when we love someone we are not easily brought to anger, but rather we overlook weaknesses or differences by feeling safe, secure, and content in the depth of the relationship.

One of the mistakes couples oftentimes make in marriage is to lose the spirit of love (and of patience) as each begins to emotionally attack the other rather than discuss a problem or situation which has arisen. Not only does this make the partner defensive, but it also whittles away at the core of that person's self-esteem. When one exercises patience in an awkward or unpleasant moment, this very act allows time to assess the situation. One can then act toward the situation, rather than react and attack the marriage partner.

As you consider patience, you should keep in mind that all successful marriages are the result of patient working and adjusting together. To suffer does not merely mean to endure pain and anguish, but as Webster states, "to allow; permit; tolerate." Growth takes some suffering. Progress and improvement in and out of marriage demands some suffering. Surely, then, you ought to invest and endure, to create beauty and joy and growth.

There are many ways in which you can show patience—to allow, permit, and tolerate—in your married life. You have perhaps heard the advice to overlook the tube of toothpaste squeezed in the middle or the socks thrown in the middle of the bedroom, and you will agree that this is usually good advice. But could you be just as patient if your mate were to become disabled? Could you tolerate your mate any longer if he were to commit adultery and beg your forgiveness? These misfortunes have happened to acquaintances of the authors, and in each instance the marriage was saved because patience and love had been learned before the misfortune struck.

On the other hand, marriages have dissolved because a husband snores or slurps his food or couldn't buy the type of house and car his wife wanted in the first two years of their marriage; or because the wife was ten pounds overweight or had a couple of wrinkles or had just celebrated her fortieth birthday.

The authors believe that couples should pay attention to the old adage "Go into marriage with both eyes wide open and afterwards keep both eyes half closed." Many couples go into marriage so starry eyed that they refuse to see the humanness of their mates. This can be good if these human frailties do not affect their salvation and if they continue to ignore them for the rest of their marriage. When they cease to tolerate the shortcomings of their spouses, however, erosions of the relationship are sure to follow.

Becoming Truly Righteous

President Spencer W. Kimball has shown that to be a loving person one must also be a righteous person.

> To be really happy in marriage, there must be a continued faithful observance of the commandments of the Lord. No one, single or married, was ever sublimely happy unless he was righteous. There are temporary satisfactions and camouflaged situations for the moment, but permanent, total happiness can come only through cleanliness and worthiness. One who has a pattern of religious life with deep religious convictions can never be happy in an inactive life. The conscience will continue to afflict unless it has been seared, in which case the marriage is already in jeopardy. A stinging conscience can make life most unbearable. Inactivity is destructive to marriage, especially where the parties are inactive in varying degrees. (*Marriage and Divorce*, pp. 23-24.)

Paul and Moroni described this part of charity with five different behaviors: (1) thinketh no evil, (2) rejoiceth not in iniquity, (3) rejoiceth in truth, (4) doth not behave itself unseemly, and (5) believeth all things. Thinking no evil means that you look for the good in yourself and others; you think of good ways to behave, and you have a pure mind. An evil person is morally corrupt and wicked. He neither edifies nor enlightens others, but instead chooses darkness and secrecy to cover his disobedient behaviors. He is destructive to faith, good morals, and godly virtues. He does not subject his behavior to principles. Instead, he is a person who "behaves unseemly" and feels laws are not applicable to him. As a result, he cannot be trusted; and without trust, his love will wither and die.

Rejoicing not in iniquity but rejoicing in truth can help your marriage immensely. It can add beauty and depth. It can help add noble things to your lives as you develop trust and unity. It can also help you avoid iniquity as you maintain a posture of obedience to God's commandments.

Believing all good things can also help your marriage. Belief is a synonym for faith throughout the scriptures. Just as belief or faith is necessary for salvation (Hebrews 10:39; D&C 20:29), belief and faith in others is necessary to be a loving person. "Faith is not to have a perfect knowledge of things; therefore if ye have faith ye hope for things which are not seen, which are true" (Alma 32:21). It takes faith in others to create the trust that is needed in marriage. It is confidence in each other that will help you throughout life's difficulties and bind you to each other.

Some couples fear rejection by those they love and so are afraid to reveal who they really are. They hide their true feelings and retreat into themselves. This lack of faith or belief in oneself and others can continually put the skids on as a person struggles to develop significant relationships. Unless you learn to believe in others, you will never learn to be a charitable or loving person.

How Can You Become More Charitable?

The first step in developing more charity is to examine yourself; and to do this you must ask yourself the following questions about your personal behavior: Am I as concerned about others as myself? Am I a patient and long-suffering person? Do I act kindly toward others? Am I hopeful and optimistic? Do I endure things well? Am I gentle, meek, and humble (teachable) as I interact with others? Am I envious of others? Do I boast or act in a "puffed up" manner? Am I easily provoked? And finally, Do I think about evil things?

If any of these behaviors is a problem for you in your relationship with your fiancé(e), you can set some specific goals—prefer-

ably in writing — about what you need to change. You may want
to discuss these goals with your fiancé(e), or you may want to
discuss a particular behavioral tendency your partner has that you
think should or could be modified as you move with your partner
toward an eternal commitment.

As a commitment is made to change, you must develop an
exact plan for making the change. This plan must be stated in
terms to include what you will do, for whom, and when the
change will take place. You then need to record (probably in your
personal journal) the progress you make in changing your
behavior.

As you have your own actions under control, you will likely
find some very exciting and rewarding things happening in your
deepening relationship. It is clearly a law of human behavior that
when we act in a certain way toward others, they have a tendency
to reciprocate by acting in a similar way toward us. When we are
harsh and defensive, others are usually harsh and defensive
toward us. When we act with mercy and kindness, we usually
receive mercy and kindness. We can label this the law of restoration in human interaction, since it is similar to the gospel law of
restoration. We will have restored to us good for good and evil for
evil. Therefore, one of the ways to increase charitable behavior in
your engagement relationship is to become a charitable fiancé(e)
by constantly thinking and performing acts of kindness.

In addition to making the above changes, there is yet another
way you can become a charitable marriage partner. It involves
how you respond to your partner's actions instead of how you
treat your partner. It is one thing to act charitable when your
fiancé(e) is being cooperative and acting charitable. It is a horse of
a different color, however, to return charity for a less than
charitable action from your fiancé(e). Those of you who truly
master this technique are living a higher law and are becoming like
the Savior.

In some circumstances the old law allowed an eye for an eye
and taught us to love our friends and to hate our enemies. The
Savior taught a higher law which is one of the greatest paradoxes
in all of human interaction. He has asked us to give back good for

evil (Matthew 5), and yet, as with all of the Savior's teachings, it works to our advantage.

While riding with a friend one day, one of the authors observed this friend accidentally moved into the next lane of traffic, thereby cutting off another car and causing the driver to swerve and slam on her brakes. The offended driver was furious and pulled alongside and yelled some very insulting remarks. It was obvious that this driver was overreacting to the incident and that she had no cause to be so rude. This seemed a perfect place to apply the law of restoration and return rudeness for rudeness. The friend, however, made a gesture to her indicating his complete apology and implying that he hoped she could still in some way have a good day. The lady was so shocked that all she could do was return his smile and drive away embarrassed for her actions.

As engagement partners you can follow this example by not allowing yourselves to simply become reactors to your partner's actions. By learning to do this prior to marriage, you can short-circuit much of the contention that may otherwise appear in your future home.

This technique can also work in a relationship where one partner is further along than the other in his or her ability to follow the Savior's rules for interacting. The best way to teach this partner to be more charitable is to use the techniques explained above. Joseph Smith taught these principles to the sisters in the Relief Society in 1842 when he said:

> Nothing is so much calculated to lead people to forsake sin as to take them by the hand, and watch over them with tenderness. When persons manifest the least kindness and love to me, O what power it has over my mind, while the opposite course has a tendency to harrow up all the harsh feelings and depress the human mind. (Joseph Smith, *Teachings of the Prophet Joseph Smith,* sel. Joseph Fielding Smith [Salt Lake City: Deseret Book Company, 1938], p. 240.)

Helping your fiancé(e) become more charitable can be done only as the Prophet Joseph suggested — with love; by first putting your own life in order and then by patiently applying the Savior's ideals for interacting.

Summary

While this section has been of an unexpected nature, it is sincerely hoped that you have gained a new perspective in one of the most vital areas of a marriage relationship. As you fashion your eternal love with charity, you will be taking a gigantic step toward beginning your marriage on the veritably loving right foot.

Use this discussion now to set the stage for the next part of the journey as you gather momentum and consider just what it will be like to begin a patriarchal relationship.

9

No power or influence can or ought to be maintained by virtue of the priesthood, only by persuasion, by long-suffering, by gentleness and meekness, and by love unfeigned. (D&C 121:41.)

Preparation for a Patriarchal Relationship

As you approach your wedding day you should do so cautiously, knowing that your island of firm footing is surrounded on all sides by the swift and changing polluted waters of the world. Many of the notions your parents and grandparents adhered to are now being questioned or discarded. You can find evidence of this in the waning tide of virtue as premarital and marital sexual attitudes and behavior are changing almost with every new day. In addition, many women are reexamining traditional roles they have been given and are finding them no longer acceptable or fulfilling.

Statements by well-known feminists challenge the traditional role of wife and mother, suggesting that women do not have equal opportunities for education or jobs and that marriage and family are instruments of women's oppression.

They speak of the beauty and sacredness of motherhood as archaic and being an inappropriate concept.

After being bombarded with statements like these, Latter-day Saint women then listen to conference addresses and hear statements such as the following by President Spencer W. Kimball:

> When men come home to their families and women devote themselves to their children, the concept will return; that to be a mother is her greatest vocation in life. She is a partner with God. No being has a position of such power and influence. She holds in her hands the destiny of nations, for to her comes the responsibility and opportunity of molding the nation's citizens. ("Why Call Me Lord, Lord, and Do Not the Things Which I Say," *Ensign*, May 1975, p. 7.)

As you can see, Latter-day Saint couples are caught in the middle of a very real and emotional tug of war to determine how they should think and act as men and women and how they should lead and follow and create equality. Hopefully, this portion of the discussion will assist you as you resolve some of these pressures and then as you walk confidently into your marriage knowing that your course has been set by truth and heavenly judgment.

An Eternal Perspective

Perhaps the first step you can take to help yourself resolve these conflicts is backward, as you purposefully back off and make sure that your basic perspective is correct. If it is not, you may be like the four blind men who were feeling the elephant to determine what elephants were like. One felt the leg, another felt the ear, another the tail, and still another the side. They each came up with a very different conclusion, not one of which was accurate and complete. As with the blind men, you must get an over-all view if you are to make sure of a correct perspective so that you can make wise decisions about both male and female roles in marriage.

Two very opposing perspectives about male-female roles dominate the controversy. One is well intentioned and partly true. Unfortunately, it is also shortsighted and partly false. It can be called the "earthly" perspective. It assumes that social roles are created only by earthly conditions, such as economic systems, traditions, migration patterns, and a gradual evolution over time. It also assumes that there is no limit to the ways roles can be modified and rearranged, whenever circumstances change—for example, whether one is living in a rural or an urban environment.

The second perspective is quite different. An eternal perspective asserts that earthly life is only a part of the eternal experience and that pre-earthly as well as post-earthly lives have an influence on the roles men and women should have. This perspective affirms that social conditions should justify some changes in roles, *but there are limits to the changes that should be made.* Some roles should not change at all, and some can change only within certain previously established limits.

These two incompatible perspectives lead to very different views of male-female roles. The earthly perspective allows people to rearrange such roles according to temporary conditions. Those who adopt this perspective see nothing wrong with radical changes, such as eliminating the distinctions between men's and women's roles in a highly industrialized society.

People in both groups can learn something from the other. Those with an earthly perspective would be better off if they were to recognize pre-earthly and post-earthly conditions, and in the long run they will make some foolish mistakes if these conditions don't influence what they do in their roles. Even so, two wrongs don't make a right; and some of those who have the eternal perspective have been more rigid than the eternal truths justify. They have sometimes forced men and women into roles that were given by the Latter-day Saint culture and have mistakenly thought that the roles were eternal. You need to recognize as a couple that there are many ways in which male-female roles can change according to customs and cultures; and you need to feel free to make the appropriate changes.

> Woman was made from the rib of man.
> She was not made from his head, to top him.
> Nor from his feet, to be stepped upon.
> She was made—

From his side, to be equal with him;
From beneath his arm, to be protected by him;
Near his heart, to be loved by him.
                                        (Author unknown.)

The Patriarchal Order

The next step you should take in recognizing the roles men and women should have in marriage is to make sure you understand the patriarchal order. You must understand that the purpose of the patriarchal order is to *create order* not to elevate one spouse above the other or to maintain servant-master roles in marriage. To create order, the partriarchal systems specifies a division of responsibility between you and your partner. Each has a specific stewardship, assigned by law and appointment, and it cannot rightfully be abdicated to the other. Because of this stewardship, both of you can know you have a place and a purpose in an eternal plan.

When properly administrated, the partriarchal family order is one of equality between husband and wife, as emphasized by President Marion G. Romney:

> They [husband and wife] should be one in harmony, respect, and mutual consideration. Neither should plan or follow an independent course of action. They should consult, pray, and decide together. . . . Remember that neither the wife nor the husband is the slave of the other. Husbands and wives are equal partners, particularly Latter-day Saint husbands and wives. They should so consider themselves and so treat each other in this life, and then they will do so throughout eternity. ("In the Image of God," *Ensign*, April 1978, pp. 2, 4.)

This statement emphasizes the equality of the marriage partners; it is not a doctrine of "sameness." It is very different from the worldly view that there are few, if any, inherent psychological and emotional differences between the sexes, that all differences are learned from our culture. This view claims that most roles now being performed by men could as easily be done by women (and vice versa) with no harm to society, children, etc. Though many roles can be given as well to men as to women, there are some basic differences that should not be ignored. Elder Boyd K. Packer has provided some unique insights into these differences:

"We recognize men and women as equally important before the Lord, but with differences biologically, emotionally, and in other ways." [First Presidency Statement on the ERA, Oct. 22, 1976.]

We cannot eliminate, through any pattern of legislation or regulation, the differences between men and women.

There are basic things that a man needs that a woman does not need. There are things that a man feels that a woman never does feel.

There are basic things that a woman needs that a man never needs, and there are things that a woman feels that a man never feels, nor should he.

These differences make women, in basic needs, literally opposite from men.

A man, for instance, needs to feel protective, and yes dominant, if you will, in leading his family. A woman needs to feel protected, in the bearing of children and in the nurturing of them.

Have you ever thought what life would be like if the needs of men and women were naturally precisely the same?

What would it be like if they both naturally needed to feel dominant all of the time, or both naturally needed to feel protected all of the time?

How disturbed and intolerable things would be.

When God created male and female, He gave each important differences in physical attributes, in emotional composition, in family responsibility. We must protect and honor the vital differences in the roles of men and women, especially in respect to the family. ("The Equal Rights Amendment," *Ensign*, March 1977, pp. 6, 7-8.)

Many in the world disagree with Elder Packer. But even so, there are many others from the scientific community who agree with him. Such a one is John H. Crook:

The biological roots of human sexual behavior are different in the two sexes and likely to be fundamental determinants in the differentiation of mature personality . . . The naive idea of a psychological "equality" of the two sexes and of their total interchangeability in the performance of social roles has gained support from certain studies purporting to demonstrate that gender role is determined simply through developmental conditioning. This view ignores totally the significance of genetic and physiological differences between the sexes that in current research are shown to exert profound effects during the behavioral maturation of the growing organism.

Those concerned with Women's Liberation would be wise to ponder the biological and psychological complementarity of the two sexes and their deep emotional needs for partnership as a counter to the notion of a poorly defined equality. (John H. Crook, *The Evolution of Human Consciousness* [Oxford: Clarendon Press, 1980], p. 242.)

While we may not yet understand in every instance which of the many differences between men and women are inherent and which are created by our cultures, it would be very unwise and premature to conclude that they do not exist.

The Husband's Role in the Patriarchal Order

The Quorum of the Twelve has provided some specific guidance as to the duties included in the role of husband-father:

Fatherhood is leadership, the most important kind of leadership. It *has* always been so, it always will be so. Father, with the assistance and counsel and encouragement of your eternal companion, you preside in the home. It is not a matter of whether you are most worthy or best qualified, but it is a matter of law and appointment. You preside at the meal table, at family prayer. You preside at family home evening, and as guided by the Spirit of the Lord, you see that your children are taught correct principles. It is your place to give direction relating to all of family life.

You give father's blessings. You take an active part in establishing family rules and discipline. As a leader in your home you plan and sacrifice to achieve the blessing of a unified and happy family. To do all of this requires that you live a family-centered life. (Council of the Twelve pamphlet, undated, p. 1-5.)

This statement does not mean that the husband is to make all of the decisions for the family. It means that the husband is to *direct the process.* You need to keep in mind President Romney's statement that neither the husband nor the wife is to plan or follow an independent course of action. They are to consult, pray, and decide together; and neither is the slave of the other. To preside does not mean to dominate and dictate, but to coordinate and to guide.

While keeping these truths in mind, you should also remember that the Lord occasionally intervenes by revealing His will. This happens in many ways, but it usually occurs through revelation to one or both spouses. When the revelation comes to only one spouse, it is important that the other spouse be willing to comply. Sometimes the revelation comes to the husband. An example of this was when the Lord spoke to father Lehi in a dream, directing him to leave Jerusalem. Even though Sariah was not enthusiastic about leaving her home at Jerusalem, still she followed the direction given to her husband. At other times the revelation may come to the wife, as when Rebekah was told why she was expecting two sons when she had previously been barren. (Genesis 25:22-23.) In this instance, the husband was supportive of the revelation given to the wife.

The Wife's Role in the Patriarchal Order

One of the questions often asked by women after reading such statements as the one by the Quorum of the Twelve is, "If the husband is to preside over and lead the family, can the wife really be considered an equal? If so, how?"

The answer has already been presented, at least partially, in this discussion. From Elder Boyd K. Packer: "We recognize men and women as equally important before the Lord, but with differences biologically, emotionally, and in other ways." From President Marion G. Romney, "Husbands and wives are equal partners." A further quotation from the Brethren will help you determine how you can be equal, even though just one presides:

> Woman does not hold the Priesthood, but she is a partaker of the blessings of the Priesthood. That is, the man holds the Priesthood, performs the priestly duties of the Church, but his wife enjoys with him every other privilege derived from the possession of the Priesthood. This is made clear, as an example, in the Temple service of the Church. The ordinances of the Temple are distinctly of Priesthood character, yet women have access to all of them, and the highest blessings of the Temple are conferred only upon the man and his wife jointly.
>
> The Prophet Joseph Smith made this relationship clear. He spoke of delivering the keys of the Priesthood to the Church, and said that the faithful members of the Relief Society should receive them with their husbands, . . .
>
> This division of responsibility is for a wise and noble purpose. Our Father in Heaven has bestowed upon His daughters a gift of

equal importance and power, which gift, if exercised in its fulness, will occupy their entire life on earth so that they can have no possible longing for that which they do not possess. The "gift" referred to is that of motherhood — the noblest, most soul-satisfying of all earthly experiences. If this power is exercised righteously, woman has no time nor desire for anything greater, for there is nothing greater on earth! This does not mean that women may not use to the full their special gifts, for . . . the more woman exercises her innate qualifications the greater is her power for motherhood. Woman may claim other activity, but motherhood should take precedence in her entire scheme of life. (John A. Widtsoe, *Priesthood and Church Government* [Salt Lake City: Deseret Book Company, 1939], pp. 83, 84.)

Without man's leadership role, he would be stripped of much of his purpose and identity. Thus there is complementarity in roles rather than similarity, coordination rather than duplication, and order rather than confusion.

Accountability

Within the family all members have an accountability for their stewardships or assigned roles. This accountability is explained in 1 Corinthians 11:3: "But I would have you know, that the head of every man is Christ; and the head of woman is the man; and the head of Christ is God."

God ◄   Christ ◄   Man ◄   Woman

From this it can be seen that the husband is not excluded from having to submit to someone who has a stewardship over him. The husband is commanded to submit himself in righteousness to the will of the Savior, and the wife is counseled to submit herself to her husband as he obeys the Son, who in turn obeys the will of the Father.

There is, however, an important qualification for submission within the patriarchal order — that of *righteousness*. The husband should have no qualms about submitting his will to the Savior's will, as Jesus Christ is always consistent and is perfect in his love and administrations, as is the Father. The wife, however, is required to submit to a mortal man who is but a god in embryo, a novice who is trying to become perfect — who has not yet arrived.

This point was disputed once by a young woman student who had been married only one week. By the end of the semester, however, she also agreed that her husband had not yet arrived at perfection. It's interesting to note that the Hebrew word for husband is *baal*, which has two meanings: (a) lord and master, and (b) *false god*. The latter meaning is probably closer to the truth much of the time.

In the meantime, what does the woman do who marries an egotistical, lord-and-master type who is in fact a spiritual midget? It would have been best not to marry him in the first place. If a husband is working on perfection, however, the woman has an obligation to help him grow spiritually. On the other hand, Brigham Young offers the following counsel:

> Mothers, remember that when your husbands are engaged in the service of the Church, and are all the time occupied in the duties of their husbands, but my counsel is — obey your husbands; and I am sanguine and most emphatic on that subject. But I never counselled a woman to follow her husband to the Devil. If a man is determined to expose the lives of his friends; let that man go to the Devil and to destruction alone. (*Discourses of Brigham Young*, comp. John A. Widtsoe [Salt Lake City: Deseret Book Company, 1954], pp. 200-201.)

Slavery, oppression, inequality, and unrighteous dominion have no part in the patriarchal order. A woman is not obligated to suffer this type of oppression. As to when enough is enough, that will have to be prayerfully considered as the problem arises.

> No power of influence can or ought to be maintained by virtue of the priesthood, only by persuasion, by long-suffering, by gentleness and meekness, and by love unfeigned. (D&C 121:41.)

Presiding in Righteousness

For the husband who desires to preside in righteousness but is not sure exactly what this means, the best guide is found in section 121 of the Doctrine and Covenants, including the verses that follow verse 41. From this revelation given to the Prophet Joseph, it is evident that most men do *not* automatically and innately know how to preside correctly. Presiding is a skill that must be learned. Undoubtedly as the Prophet Joseph increased his understanding of this while imprisoned in the Liberty Jail, he impressed not to conclude by stating that most of us cannot lead in righteousness. He taught that there are basically ten ways to lead properly in the patriarchal order and in other priesthood roles. These are listed below with the authors' comments:

1. *Persuasion.* This is probably the chief tool of priesthood leadership. It means an attempt to convince our spouses and families through the presentation of ideas and concepts. It is the opposite of force or tyranny. It is talking and reasoning—without raising our voices or threatening. It is sharing ideas to show others the wisdom in what we desire. Whenever we use *persuasion,* the other person is free to agree or to disagree, according to his free agency.

2. *Long-suffering.* Patience and a willingness to overlook imperfections in our mates are important parts of priesthood leadership. Long-suffering is the opposite of impatience, fault-finding, and expecting perfectionism.

3. *Gentleness.* A gentle husband is one who respects his wife and considers her his equal. A gentle husband is sensitive to his wife's needs, both emotional and physical, and is never guilty of forcing his own desires upon her.

4. *Meekness.* To be meek is to be teachable and willing to conform to gospel standards and thus submit our will to the will of the Lord. The meek husband is not a law unto himself. He cares about others' feelings and is willing to be taught by them.

5. *Love unfeigned.* An unfeigned love is one that is sincere, not counterfeit or hypocritical. It is genuine. We do not love our mates simply for what they can do for us; we love them as persons of unique worth, in and of themselves. Their lives are as important to us as our own lives.

6. *Kindness.* Kindness is an attitude which should moderate the actions of priesthood leadership at all times. It is the opposite of cruelty, revenge, and being nonforgiving. The highest form of kindness we can show others is to forgive them completely.

7. *Pure knowledge.* To preside with pure knowledge is to lead one's family by revelation and inspiration. Pure knowledge comes from God and is undefiled and unpolluted with the theories of

men. How fortunate is the family that has a patriarch at its head who is able to use this gift to bless his family!

8. *No hypocrisy.* The father-husband within the patriarchal order should not be guilty of requiring his wife and family to sacrifice, work, go the extra mile, do without wants or necessities, forego recreation or hobbies, etc., if he himself is not willing to live by the same rules. There cannot be two codes of conduct based on the assumption that the one spouse has an inherent right to more privileges than the others.

9. *No guile.* To lead guilefully is to lead with deceitful cunning, by duplicity (or doubleness) of thought, speech, or action. There is no place for this type of presiding within a true patriarchal order. To see as we are seen and know as we are known is to be without guile and to be completely genuine.

10. *Charity.* Charity is the pure love of Christ; it is an essential character trait of the patriarchal leader. Couples who manifest charity are promised confidence, understanding, and the constant companionship of the Holy Ghost, and an everlasting dominion of righteousness and truth (D&C 121:45-56).

Methods of Presiding and Following

As you prepare for marriage you should appreciate the fact that within the patriarchal order there is some flexibility as to how a husband presides and how a wife submits to his leadership. The Lord has provided some guidelines, some do's and don'ts; but to live within the bounds of the order is not to be "commanded in all things." In fact, individual differences are desirable and even essential as long as you stay within the bounds the Lord has set. The rest of this chapter discusses several techniques that couples have found useful in working out their own styles of presiding and following. It is likely that you, as an engaged couple, can identify additional ideas you will find useful.

Presiding and Conducting Are Different

While the difference between presiding and conducting is readily understood in Church meetings, many Latter-day Saints blur and confuse the distinction in their homes.

The presiding responsibilities are not passed around or rotated in a priesthood organization. One person is always identified as the one to preside; and whenever that person is present, he or she is presiding. If that person is absent, another person is identified as the one to temporarily preside. Since the patriarchal order in a family makes it a priesthood organization, this same procedure should be followed. The father should preside, and this function should be delegated to others only when he is absent.

Conducting, on the other hand, is quite different. The person who is conducting a particular function takes the initiative to organize things, get things going, direct activities to make sure they run smoothly, and stop things at the appropriate time. The person conducting is the one who speaks up and actually manages the operations. Conducting is done under the direction of the one who is presiding, but the presiding role can be passive much of the time.

Looking down the road a little, you can foresee a growing family with teenage sons holding the priesthood. In such a case, who presides when the husband and father is absent? Here is a quotation from the Relief Society Manual, 1974-75:

> Recently a good sister wrote to President Spencer W. Kimball of the Council of the Twelve, asking him who should preside in the home when the father is absent. The letter was referred to the First Presidency for the answer. The following is from their reply: 'You inquire as to who presides in the home when the husband is absent, whether it is the mother or the oldest member of the family holding the priesthood. I am directed to tell you that the mother is the presiding authority in the home when the husband is absent.'

Delegate and Report

Those who are familiar with priesthood quorums recognize that the dual process of delegating and then reporting is an important part of priesthood activities. In delegating, the person who is conducting asks someone to take an assignment. The assignment is an agreement to do something, to perform a specific task. The person receiving the assignment may have volunteered for or been asked to accept the assignment. There is also a provision for the person who gave the assignment. If it can be completed in a short period of time, the person usually reports back after the job is completed. If the assignment is a long-term responsibility, the person periodically reports on how things are going with his stewardship.

It is important to realize that the process of delegating and reporting is more than just a convenient way to get things done. It is the method the Lord used in heaven before the earth was created, the method He uses now, and the method He will likely use in the future. It is, therefore, an eternal way of organizing things, and you would do well to learn how to use it in your marriage. The way to proceed is for you to begin early in your marriage to follow the example of the scriptures by having family councils to decide how to organize yourselves. "And the Gods took counsel among themselves and said: let us . . ." (Abraham 4:26).

You can learn to counsel together even before you marry, deciding who should have which tasks in your marriage system. This should never be a process in which the husband tells the wife what she ought to do, in which the husband gets his way more than she does, or in which the husband gets the last word. *These are not priesthood privileges.* The husband and wife should talk and come to a mutually satisfactory agreement about how to organize themselves. If this means that the wife conducts family councils because she likes to and is good at it, so be it. If it means that the wife mows the lawn and the husband does the laundry, so be it. If it means that the husband has the most say with buying cars and recreational equipment, while the wife has the most say about buying furniture and houses, so be it. And if you decide to organize your family in a way that is very different from both your parents' families, so be it.

The key in this process is to remember that the husband presides over the family as a whole. This means he *directs the process* of family and married life. He does not get his way more than others. In fact, he may get his way less often, because he needs to sacrifice for the whole. He is not a dictator, and he is not the boss. He has a God-given assignment to make sure that the family system operates with order, and he is to do it by patience, request, love, suggestions; by asking others to accept assignments and receiving reports about the assignment so he knows how things are going; by occasionally conducting meetings himself; by encouraging others; and by respecting the rights and wishes of those around him. Recognizing that the greatest among us is a servant, he willingly serves.

Lead With Softness

A beautiful example of how to preside was given by Spencer W. Kimball. In at least one situation wherein he was presiding over a meeting in the temple, rather than tell the others that he would give the prayer, he asked, "Is it all right if I give the prayer?" (Personal correspondence.) He asked those over whom he presided, rather than just told them. It was a gentle request, rather than an instruction or order. The difference between gentleness and force, between softness and coercion, is so small and yet so great. How often did the Lord speak of being merciful, kind, peacemaking, forgiving, gentle, and loving? How much should we act in these ways as we preside — and follow?

President Kimball has suggested that we have "a style of our own." This applies in the way we preside and follow in our homes. We ought to adopt the style advocated by the Savior — of patience, mercy, kindness, love unfeigned, and softness. Were this to occur, we would find much more joy and peace than most of us ever thought possible.

Allow for Agency

One of the difficult challenges when presiding is to find the proper balance between the interests of the individuals in a group and those of the group as a whole. As an individual, a person should be able to exercise his own free agency, and yet he cannot have complete freedom because excessive freedom may interfere with the rights of others.

When children are small, they are given little freedom simply because they lack wisdom and experience. They are told what time to go to bed, what time to get up, what to eat, etc. As these children grow up, two things change. They are allowed more and more freedom, and their parents gradually learn to change the methods they use to induce compliance. Parents learn to ask more and tell less, to make suggestions and give advice; and the children are gradually allowed enough freedom and independence that they can choose to accept or reject suggestions and advice.

Allowing for agency is more complex in your marriage relationship simply because you are both adults. You both want and deserve certain freedoms and independence, and occasionally you may want freedoms that interfere with your marriage or your family life.

What do you do then?

There are no simple solutions to this dilemma, but there are several things that are good to remember. First, both extremes are bad. You can have too little or too much freedom. Second, most people in our modern culture err in allowing too little freedom to those around them. They want them to do things their way. They want too much control over what their spouses and older children want to do. They need to recognize that those around them need to make choices and to learn by the good and bad decisions they make.

Summary

This section has centered around the fundamental parts of the patriarchal order and has described several things that you could do to use this system of government wisely. The patriarchal order provides a division of labor wherein the man is to preside in the family and the woman is to give birth to the children and have the primary responsibility for rearing the children. In both areas the other spouse is to assist. This creates a harmonious complementarity that does not elevate one sex above the other. Both have crucial responsibilities. This provides order and equality, but not sameness.

There is considerable freedom in the way you can administer the patriarchal order in your home. The presiding member is to *direct the process* in the home rather than to always have his way. He is to make sure that things get done; and the best way to accomplish this is to be a gentle leader who gets consensus about decisions, makes assignments, delegates responsibilities, and monitors what is happening to determine when new decisions need to be made. He is, therefore, a steward, a servant, and a manager, rather than a drill sergeant or dictator. The methods that he should employ are gentleness, persuasion, kindness, love, encouragement, affection, and softness.

Press onward now, faithful reader, and taste the excitement of preparing for "your" day in the House of the Lord.

More butterflies are felt,
more tears shed and prayers
said, and more joy experienced
on our wedding day than on any
other single day in our lives.
(Brenton G. Yorgason.)

10

Preparing to Go to the Temple

Well . . . here you are, beginning the last leg of your journey toward marriage, preparing for your day in the temple. As you prepare yourself, what can you expect? What goes on in the temple? And what should you do now to be ready for the temple?

Why Have Temples?

The temple, as you know, is a very special and sacred place, much different from other buildings. Temples are reserved for activities that are so sacred that only those who are living to certain prescribed standards are admitted to them.

Having sacred places wherein only the righteous could go to worship, make covenants with our Heavenly Father, and renew the covenants is not restricted to this day and age. The Lord has always reserved certain places for His holy work. Moses was asked to remove his shoes because "the place whereon thou standest is holy ground" (Exodus 3:5). In addition, only the High Priest was allowed into the holiest part of the ancient Israelite temple (Leviticus 16:2-4).

The Lord tells us that He has temples so He can, in His words,

> reveal mine ordinances therein unto my people; For I deign to reveal unto my church things which have been kept hid from before the foundation of the world. (D&C 124:40-41.)

Speaking further of temple work, its special revelations and ordinances, the Lord said:

> Therefore, verily I say unto you, that your anointings, and your washings, and your baptisms for the dead, and your solemn assemblies, . . . and for your oracles in your most holy places wherein you receive conversations, . . . and for the glory, honor, and endowment of all her municipals. (D&C 124:39.)

Thus, the temples are special places wherein you can go to receive information, make covenants, worship, and receive special blessings.

Temple Ordinances

When you go to the temple, you should expect to participate in ordinances that will help prepare you for the culminating experience of being sealed as husband and wife for all eternity. One of these ordinances is called the *endowment*. Brigham Young described the endowment in the following way:

> Your *endowment* is, to receive all those ordinances in the House of the Lord, which are necessary for you, after you have departed this life, to enable you to walk back to the presence of the Father, passing the angels who stand as sentinels, being enabled to give them the key words, the signs and tokens, pertaining to the Holy Priesthood, and gain your eternal exaltation in spite of earth and hell. (*Journal of Discourses*, 26 vols. [London: Latter-day Saints' Book Depot, 1854-86], 2:31.)

The endowment, an experience that lasts several hours, is a combination of receiving information and instructions pertaining to the plan of salvation and exaltation and of making covenants to live in accordance with the principles taught in the temple. In the endowment ceremony, as in other ordinances, principles of the gospel are taught largely through symbolism. Previous experiences such as baptism and the sacrament are symbolic. For example, in baptism our burial in the water is symbolic of the Savior's burial in the tomb, and our rising from the water is symbolic of the Resurrection. The water is also symbolic of being cleansed from sin and raised to newness of life. The bread and water in the sacrament are symbolic of the body and blood of the Savior. Many new symbols are learned in the sacred endowment in the temple.

The endowment covers many aspects of the gospel that are discussed in the scriptures. To be well prepared you may wish to study the following scriptures thoroughly: Moses 2:1 to 5:8; D&C 124:36-41; D&C 132:15-24; D&C 59:3-8; D&C 130:11; Alma 22:7-14.

The Sealing

After you and your fiancé(e) have received your endowments, you are then ready to be sealed as husband and wife for eternity. There are special rooms in the temples that are referred to as sealing rooms wherein this sacred ordinance is performed. As with all sacred ordinances, the sealing ceremony has a quiet, simple dignity. It is very different from some of the gaudy and ornate traditions of the world in which the emphasis is on the pomp and ceremony. The ceremony centers around covenants which you will make with each other and with the Lord. It is a sacred rather than spectacular moment when you both humble yourselves before the altar of the Lord and are sealed for time and for all eternity by the holy priesthood of God.

Some Frequently Asked Questions

The temple endowment has so much new information that you will not fully understand it the first time you go through an endowment session. Also, some of the symbolism has new ideas and new meanings. This means that you will likely have many questions about many things. There will be an opportunity in the temple for you to ask questions, and those who accompany you to the temple can help you learn and grow. Many of these questions cannot be discussed here because the ordinances are so sacred that they should be revered to the extent that they are dealt with only in the proper place — that is, within the sacred and uplifting and beautifully peaceful surroundings of the House of the Lord.

There are many questions that engaged couples have. For example, some wonder about the temple garment. "What is its significance and value?" "Why do we wear it?" Yet another question, "If I have other questions about the temple before I go or while I am there, where can I turn to receive the answers?" These questions can be answered by consulting with your bishop or branch president. He will provide all of the information you will need. In addition, when you are in the temple, there are individuals assigned to assist you. You will never be left unattended on your first temple visit; and helpful and courteous temple workers will be available on later visits whenever you need assistance.

Another question that is often asked is, "Why do I need to go back to the temple after receiving my endowment?" Elder John A. Widtsoe answered this question in the following way:

> It is not expected that the temple ceremonies can be comprehended in full detail the first time a person "goes through" the temple. Therefore, the Lord has provided means of repetition. Temple work must be done first by each person for himself or herself; then it may be done for one's dead ancestors or friends. . . . This service will open the doors of salvation for the dead and will also help fix upon the mind of the living the nature, meaning, and obligations of the endowment. ("Look Toward the Temple," *Temples of The Church of Jesus Christ of Latter-day Saints* [Salt Lake City: The Church of Jesus Christ of Latter-day Saints, 1979], p. 78.)

A Word About the Covenants You Will Make

The term *covenant* has been used many times in this discussion and it has a special meaning in the gospel. It is more than just a promise or agreement. An agreement can be changed whenever the parties involved want to change it. A promise can also be changed. All you need to do is get the consent of the person to whom you've made the promise, and it can be modified or eliminated. A covenant is different, very different.

There are two things that make it different. First, it involves something that is sacred, and this means that the Lord is always involved. Notice that this is always true with the two different types of covenants. The Lord can covenant that He will do something. We can covenant with the Lord that we will do something. This makes a covenant a spiritual and sacred agreement.

The second characteristic of an eternal covenant is that it is a permanent agreement. A marriage not entered into by covenant lasts only until the grave. The Lord's form of marriage is a covenant, an everlasting covenant (D&C 131), because it is to last beyond the grave.

Before you are spiritually ready for marriage, you need to be ready to make the kind of commitment that is permanent. You are not agreeing that you will stay married as long as the other person is young and beautiful and you are romantically in love. You are not saying that you will stay married as long as everything is pleasant and you do not have serious problems and differences. You *are* agreeing that you are ready to make a permanent commitment to a marriage.

Consider, if you will, the following:

Some may wonder why the Lord gives commandments and requires us to enter into covenants with him. Or, as one person asked: "If the Lord loves us, why does he give us commandments? If he loves us, why does he say 'Thou shalt' or 'Thou shalt not'?"

A simple answer to these questions is, he commands us because he loves us. He knows perfectly well what will bring us peace and success in our individual lives and in the world and what will bring the opposite.

Just as any father would direct (or even restrict) his children . . . so our Father in heaven gives us commandments, laws, and covenants, not for the sole purpose of restricting us or burdening us, but rather that we may, through obedience to correct principles, find peace and success.

Actually, we do not *have* to do what the Lord commands us, but we cannot obtain the rewards and blessings he has promised unless we do.

"For all who will have a blessing at my hands shall abide the law which was appointed for that blessing, and the conditions thereof, as were instituted from before the foundation of the world." (D&C 132:5.)

> Every member of the Church has made covenants with the Lord. These commandments and covenants are not grievous; they are not burdensome. On the contrary, they are enlightening, uplifting, assuring, and helpful. They are instruments of voluntary action on our part that help us to concentrate our efforts to accomplish the purpose of life and to reach our ultimate goal. (ElRay L. Christiansen, "We Have Made Covenants with the Lord," *Ensign,* Jan. 1973, pp. 50-51.)

Thus, if you are not capable of keeping covenants, you are not capable of receiving the blessings that will come with a happy, eternal marriage. The following statements by the First Presidency illustrate the importance of your being ready for these obligations:

> Applicants in too many cases seem to be more appreciative of going through the House of the Lord than deeply conscious of the obligations they take upon themselves by so doing. (First Presidency letter, August 23, 1941.)

> It should be remembered that men and women who go through the temple should be so seasoned in the Gospel and Church work, that the temple ordinances confer not only blessings, but impose obligations. . . . It is far wiser and better for members to postpone taking on these obligations and entering into these covenants until they are so thoroughly seasoned and informed in the Gospel that they can keep the covenants than it is to go into the temple and make these sacred promises and then come out and repudiate them. (First Presidency letter, October 18, 1950.)

There have been enough unfortunate examples of Latter-day Saints who have gone to the temple before they should have to make such statements by the First Presidency necessary. One such couple known to the authors married young and out of the temple, much to the embarrassment of both parents. The parents were anxious for their children to go to the temple as soon as possible and did everything in their power to persuade them. After many futile efforts the parents finally decided to offer the couple a modest house as a reward if they would have their marriage sealed in the temple. The young couple accepted the bribe and became active long enough to be able to get a temple recommend and to be sealed for time and all eternity. Unfortunately, the couple were not spiritually mature enough to keep the covenants that they had entered into and have since fallen back into inactivity . . . and all the while placing condemnation upon their heads for living contrary to the covenants they have made.

Why Is It Important to Be Married in the Temple?

Many benefits come from a temple marriage. You will receive some of them immediately, in your earthly experience. Others are received in the future. One advantage of being married in the temple is that you will then *view* your marriage as an eternal unit with an eternal commitment. This will help you have motivation to work through the small differences and obstacles that you encounter in life. The result is that your marriage will be more enjoyable than it would likely have been without this extra commitment.

Another advantage is that you will view your temple marriage as a sacred arrangement. It is more than just a personal commitment, a social arrangement, or part of an institutionalized system. It is a revered and precious part of your life. This will give your marriage relationship a special dignity and lofty status that it would lack if you were married "for time only" out of the temple.

There are also a number of advantages to a temple marriage that are subtle and spiritual. Some of them are summarized in the following observations by Church leaders:

> Those married in the temple in the new and everlasting covenant of marriage become inheritors of all the blessings of Abraham, Isaac, and Jacob and all the patriarchs and thereby enter into the patriarchal order. If the participating parties abide in the eternal marriage covenant, they shall reap the full blessings of patriarchal heirship in eternity where the patriarchal order will be the order of government and rule. (*Mormon Doctrine*, p. 559.)

> The Lord has given unto us privileges, and blessings, and the opportunity of entering into covenants, of accepting ordinances that pertain to our salvation beyond what is preached in the world; beyond the 'principles of faith in the Lord Jesus Christ, repentance from sin, and baptism for the remission of sins, and the laying on

of hands for the gift of the Holy Ghost; and these principles and covenants are received nowhere else but in the temple of God.

If you would become a son or a daughter of God and an heir of the kingdom, then you must go to the house of the Lord and receive blessings which there can be obtained and which cannot be obtained elsewhere; and you must keep those commandments and those covenants to the end. . . . (Joseph Fielding Smith, *Doctrines of Salvation*, 3 vols. [Salt Lake City: Bookcraft, 1954-56], 2:40.)

Preparing to Go to the House of the Lord

There are many things you can do as you prepare to receive your endowment and be sealed in the House of the Lord. The most important thing is to live the basic teachings of the gospel of Jesus Christ. Then, when you feel worthy, you can schedule an interview with your bishop or branch president to obtain a temple recommend. Elder Boyd K. Packer in his book *The Holy Temple* wrote:

> The interview for a temple recommend is conducted privately between the bishop and the Church member concerned. Here the member is asked searching questions about his personal conduct and worthiness and about his loyalty to the Church and its officers. The person must certify that he is morally clean and is keeping the Word of Wisdom, paying a full tithing, living in harmony with the teachings of the Church, and not maintaining any affiliation or sympathy with apostate groups. The bishop is instructed that confidentiality in handling these matters with each interviewee is of the utmost importance. (Salt Lake City: Bookcraft, 1980, p. 53.)

If worthy, you will be given a certificate that indicates to the clerk at the door of the temple that you are worthy to enter. If you are not ready to enter the temple after you have had your interview, you can counsel with your bishop or branch president about what you will need to do to become such. He will work out with you a program to help you improve your worthiness.

In addition to being worthy enough to obtain a recommend, you will want to do several other things. You will want to prepare your mind and your spirit by regularly reading in the scriptures and learning how to worship and draw close to our Heavenly Father. You will want to learn how to pray in a way that you feel close to the Holy Spirit. This, of course, means that you will pray more than just the routine prayers—such as before a meal and in meetings. You will want to learn how to pray for many minutes as you express your gratitude for the many blessings you have. As you begin doing this, you will learn what the Lord meant when He said, "He that hath ears to hear, let him hear" (Matthew 11:15). You will learn that you have spiritual ears that "hear" just as surely as do your physical ears. They don't hear sound waves. They hear spiritual messages. And, just like any other part of your body, the more you use them, the stronger they become and the more you can hear with them. On the other hand, the less you use them, the less you can hear with them. As you strengthen your spiritual senses, you will be preparing yourself to receive the greatest blessings of your life within the temple of the Lord.

In Conclusion

Well, here you are! This has been a long journey as you have wound your way through the chapters of this book. And yet, hopefully, it has been enjoyable and rewarding as well as thought provoking, as you have considered the many and varied aspects within the marriage relationship. As you can see, the LDS concept of what a marriage is really all about is much more involved than merely a secular wedding. In the Doctrine and Covenants the Lord instructs His children that "unto whom much is given much is *required*" (D&C 82:3, italics added). As a young Latter-day Saint, you have been blessed more than any other people who have lived on this earth, and because of this He *requires* a lofty standard of conduct from you.

As authors, we salute you for remaining steadfast and un-compromising in your pursuit of an eternally rewarding marriage. We wish you the very greatest of blessings as you prepare for *your* day . . . and always.

Index